Advocating for Nonresident Fathers in Child Welfare Court Cases

Andrew L. Cohen

Richard Cozzola

Kathleen Creamer

Judge Leonard P. Edwards (ret.)

Daniel L. Hatcher

Mark S. Kiselica

Jennifer L. Renne

Vivek S. Sankaran

Andrya L. Soprych

Publication Directors: *Jessica R. Kendall and Lisa Pilnik*

Edited by *Claire S. Chiamulera*

Center on Children and the Law

AMERICAN BAR ASSOCIATION

NATIONAL QUALITY IMPROVEMENT CENTER
ON NON-RESIDENT FATHERS AND THE CHILD WELFARE SYSTEM

Copyright © 2009 American Bar Association and American Humane Association

ISBN-10: 1-60442-589-x
ISBN-13: 978-1-60442-589-5

This book was made possible through a cooperative agreement between the U.S. Department of Health and Human Services, Administration for Children and Families, Children's Bureau, the American Humane Association, the American Bar Association Center on Children and the Law, and the National Fatherhood Initiative.

Library of Congress Cataloging-in-Publication Data

Advocating for nonresident fathers in child welfare court cases / Andrew L. Cohen ... [et al.] ; edited by Claire S. Chiamulera.

    p. cm.
  ISBN 978-1-60442-589-5
    1. Fathers—Legal status, laws, etc.—United States. 2. Parent and child (Law)—United States. 3. Father and child—United States. I. Cohen, Andrew L., 1965- II. Sandt, Claire.
  KF547.A935 2009
  346.7301'7—dc22

Portions of this book appeared in a different format in *ABA Child Law Practice*, published by the ABA Center on Children and the Law.

The quotations from fathers found in this book have been reprinted with permission from the National Fatherhood Initiative.

The Shaine Yates story was adapted with permission from an article that appeared in the spring 2009 issue of *QIC News*, published by the National Quality Improvement Center on Non-Resident Fathers and the Child Welfare System.

Graphic design by Zaccarine Design, Inc., Evanston, IL

Nonresident fathers *are men whose children are involved in the child welfare system, but who did not live with their children when the suspected abuse or neglect occurred. They are also often referred to as noncustodial fathers.*

Contents

Foreword

Engaging nonresident fathers in the child welfare system is critical, yet few fathers who become involved have a positive experience. Most say that they don't understand what is expected of them, and that the system makes them jump through hoops to see their kids. They don't understand why they are looked at with suspicion or why placing their children with complete strangers is better than letting their "kids come home" with them. They become frustrated and angry with "the system," causing them and their children to lose out.

Nonresident fathers need a guide to help them navigate the child welfare system. They need an advocate who knows the system, can stay calm under pressure, and has the desire to look out for their rights and the tools to do so.

Choosing this book means you have the desire to be a guide for nonresident fathers. Reading it will increase your knowledge and give you the tools to advocate for nonresident fathers effectively. You will learn how to:

- make constitutional arguments that protect nonresident fathers' legal rights;
- work with male clients and forge meaningful relationships with them;
- advocate for fathers in and out of the courtroom to protect their legal rights to achieve and maintain meaningful relationships with their children;
- address special legal issues, such as domestic violence, immigration, child support, and incarceration; and
- address tough ethical challenges that arise when representing nonresident fathers.

Research shows that the more engaged the nonresident father is the better the outcomes for the child. It's your job to help fathers take responsibility and become engaged with their children, the child welfare system and the courts. It will not be easy, but it might make the difference in the life of a father and most importantly, in the life of a child.

Howard A. Davidson, Director
ABA Center on Children and the Law

Acknowledgements

This book is a product of the National Quality Improvement Center on Non-Resident Fathers and the Child Welfare System (QIC NRF), funded by the Children's Bureau of the U.S. Department of Health and Human Services. We are grateful to our Project Officer, Jason Bohn, and to our QIC NRF project partners, American Humane Association and National Fatherhood Initiative, for their support and thoughtful feedback on our draft manuscripts. We thank the authors for their hard work and effective advocacy on behalf of fathers, and Shaine Yates and the other fathers who shared their stories with us. Howard Davidson, the ABA Center on Children and the Law's Director, and Richard Cozzola, a member of the National Advisory Board for the QIC NRF reviewed drafts of this book and provided useful insights and suggestions. Mark Hardin shaped and informed our early thinking and focus on this subject. Scott Raub and Julie Hillman, legal interns, provided invaluable research assistance and developed several of the materials in the appendices to this book.

Claire S. Chiamulera
Jessica R. Kendall
Lisa Pilnik

Introduction

As a lawyer representing a parent in the child welfare system, you may feel like David facing Goliath. Courts often favor the child welfare agency position, and you often lack resources and assistance to adequately represent indigent clients with multiple problems. Representing parents in child protection cases requires expertise in child welfare practice and strong advocacy skills, both in and out of court. Representing noncustodial (i.e., nonresident) fathers is complex and presents unique factual and legal issues.

As a judge hearing a case where a father has not been located or is not engaged, you may feel that critical information and resources are missing. You may be concerned about fathers who have not played much of a role for their children. You may also struggle to engage them in meaningful ways.

This book is your guide to advocating for and engaging nonresident fathers whose children are in the child welfare system. These men are often a silent or missing party from child welfare courtrooms. Judges with hundreds of cases before them report that they remember vividly the nonresident fathers with whom they have placed children—because it rarely happens. Nonresident fathers are an underused resource in the child welfare system. Even if they can't or shouldn't assume physical custody of their child, they are important people in their children's lives. They can contribute in many ways, including opening the door to paternal family resources that may have been unknown, and influencing their future academic and employment success.

Unfortunately the child welfare system (by practice and sometimes policy) often shuts out nonresident fathers, even when they have never been accused of perpetrating abuse. Services are rarely offered or geared towards them. Child welfare agency case staffings or case plans rarely include them. In some jurisdictions, they may not assume custody without first proving they are fit parents.

Many noncustodial fathers fear any court system involvement, even if it means losing contact with their children. Some face personal obstacles, such as poverty, joblessness, or mental health or substance abuse issues that prevent them from fully participating in their children's lives. Some have prior criminal histories, or unfulfilled child support orders. They need strong and sustained advocacy from the beginning of their child's case through permanency, to ensure their voices are heard, and their goals of involvement with their children are met. Both can positively impact their child's case in terms of safety, permanency, and well-being.

Each chapter of this book is written by an expert in the field and gives you the tools to successfully incorporate fathers into child welfare cases.

- **Chapter 1:** Vivek Sankaran writes about Supreme Court precedent on this issue and how different states have interpreted it, while providing tips to lawyers on preserving fathers' rights.

- **Chapter 2:** Mark Kiselica explores how to establish a good working relationship with father clients and how to make men feel comfortable engaging in the child welfare system.

- **Chapter 3:** Richard Cozzola and Andrya Soprych detail how to advocate for father clients outside of court. The authors provide guidance on how to advocate for and counsel a father through agency case staffings to obtain needed assistance and develop and achieve case goals.

- **Chapter 4:** Andrew Cohen looks at how to help a father realize his goals through the court process. He shares strategies to use at adjudication, permanency hearings, and termination of parental rights hearings to help fathers maintain regular contact with their children.

- **Chapter 5:** Judge Leonard Edwards discusses how judges can better engage fathers at all stages of a child welfare case. He details effective engagement strategies and offers sample courtroom dialogues and court orders to foster engagement.

- **Chapter 6:** Andrew Cohen discusses how to address special issues that may interfere with a father's involvement in his child's case, including domestic violence, substance abuse, immigration issues, and mental health problems.

- **Chapter 7:** Daniel Hatcher shares strategies to ensure fathers' child support obligations do not prevent or scare them away from meaningfully engaging with their child and the child's court case.

- **Chapter 8:** Kathleen Creamer offers guidance on representing incarcerated fathers and explains how to help them maintain relationships with their children and participate in court proceedings, even if they can't attend in person.

- **Chapter 9:** Jennifer Renne describes common ethical dilemmas for lawyers representing nonresident fathers in child welfare proceedings. She also discusses potential conflicts of interest when representing multiple fathers and what it means to diligently and zealously represent a father.

Complimenting these chapters are:

- **Chapter checklists** highlighting key practice strategies for each chapter.

- **Shaine's story** describing a nonresident father's struggle to gain custody of his child through child welfare proceedings.

- **Sample questions** and a **lawyer's checklist** to assess whether a father has established a constitutionally protected relationship with his child.

- **Interstate placement guidance** when the father lives out of state.

- **First meeting tips** offering guidance to lawyers when meeting a father for the first time.

- **Ten tips for working with your lawyer**, a handout to give father clients to foster the lawyer-client relationship.

Federal and state governments are starting to acknowledge the important roles fathers play in their children's lives. This book is the first of its kind, focusing exclusively on representing and engaging nonresident fathers—a group who remain undervalued and underserved in the child welfare system. In addition to guiding lawyers and judges who work with these fathers, it seeks to promote increased father involvement in these cases to achieve better outcomes for children and families.

Jessica R. Kendall and Lisa Pilnik
ABA Center on Children and the Law

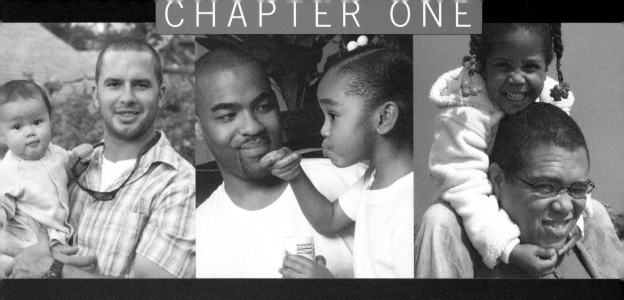

CHAPTER ONE

Advocating for the Constitutional Rights of Nonresident Fathers

Vivek S. Sankaran

CHECKLIST

Advocating for the Constitutional Rights of Nonresident Fathers

Determine if your client has a constitutionally protected interest in his child.

➤ Find out if your client has or has attempted to establish a relationship with his child that gives him a right to notice and an opportunity to be heard in court proceedings.

➤ Assess whether he has perfected this interest by determining if he has complied with the state's procedures to establish paternity, such as:

  ➤ filing with a putative father registry;

  ➤ placing his name on the birth certificate;

  ➤ being married to the mother at the time of conception or birth;

  ➤ maintaining regular contact and a relationship with the child; and/or

  ➤ paying child support.

File necessary pleadings to safeguard your client's constitutional rights.

➤ Has your nonoffending, nonresident father client been denied custody and forced to comply with services, absent proof of unfitness? If so, the state may be encroaching upon his constitutionally protected interests.

➤ If the father's constitutional interests are not being protected, consider:

  ➤ filing a motion challenging the imposition of services;

  ➤ arguing that the court can't interfere with his constitutionally protected custodial rights;

  ➤ requesting immediate placement of the child with the father.

Understand the interplay between state law and constitutional rights.

➤ Generally, between state and federally based rights, legal fathers should be able to:

  ➤ be notified of proceedings;

  ➤ visit their children;

  ➤ request custody;

  ➤ receive court-appointed counsel, if indigent; and

  ➤ have a hearing before their parental rights are terminated.

Download this and other checklists at **www.fatherhoodqic.org/checklists**

M onths after a child welfare case is petitioned, a nonresident father appears in court and requests custody of his children who are living in foster care. Little is known about the father, and immediately, the system—judge, caseworkers, and lawyers—view him with suspicion and caution, inquiring about his whereabouts and his prior involvement in the children's lives. Those doubts, in turn, raise complicated questions about his legal rights to his children.

- Does the Constitution give him any rights to his children and is he entitled to a presumption of parental fitness?
- Did he preserve those rights?
- Does state law grant him stronger protections?
- Is the court permitted to place the children in foster care if no allegations of unfitness are made against him?

As a lawyer or judge working in the child welfare system, you're likely to face this scenario. The largest percentage of child victims of abuse and neglect come from households headed by single mothers. Consequently, dependency proceedings frequently focus on reunifying children with their mothers.[1] The child welfare system responds to this dynamic by treating fathers as legal strangers to their children and minimizing the importance of their rights. Often, involving fathers is an afterthought. Evidence reveals that child welfare caseworkers, courts, and lawyers typically do a poor job locating nonresident fathers at the outset of a case, involving them once identified, and ensuring their constitutional and statutory rights are fully protected.[2]

But a growing consensus has emerged that disempowering fathers in this way harms children, who generally benefit when both parents participate in their lives.[3] Efforts are underway across the country to transform child welfare systems to recognize rights of fathers and develop practices and procedures to help them participate in the child welfare process.

This chapter offers guidance to help legal advocates protect nonresident fathers' constitutional rights. After briefly reviewing parents' constitutional rights, it provides a framework to assess whether a nonresident father has perfected these rights and taken steps to preserve them. It then discusses states' efforts to adjudicate the rights of nonresident fathers and encourages lawyers to determine if those efforts are constitutional. Zealous advocacy will help ensure the child welfare system validates the meaningful relationships between nonresident fathers and their children.

Nonresident Father Involvement in Dependency Cases

In a multistate study, researchers conducted telephone interviews with 1,222 caseworkers in Arizona, Massachusetts, Minnesota, and Tennessee. Caseworkers were interviewed about 1,958 children in their caseloads, each of whom had a living father who did not reside in the household from which the child was removed. The study found:

➤ 72% of caseworkers noted that paternal involvement enhanced child well-being.

➤ 68% of fathers were identified by the caseworker.

➤ 55% of fathers were actually contacted by the caseworker.

➤ 50% of those fathers contacted expressed interest in their child living with them.

➤ 56% of contacted fathers (30% of all fathers in the study) visited their child.

➤ 50% of contacted fathers (28% of all fathers in the study) expressed interest in assuming custody of their child.

➤ 4% of cases involving nonresident fathers had a goal of reunification with the father.

Source:
Malm K., J. Murray and R. Geen. *What about the Dads? Child Welfare Agencies' Efforts to Identify, Locate and Involve Nonresident Fathers.* Washington, D.C.: U.S. Department of Health and Human Services, Office of the Assistant Secretary for Planning and Evaluation, 2006. Available at: http://aspe.hhs.gov/hsp/06/CW-involve-dads/index.htm.

Preserving Fathers' Constitutional Rights

Your first task is to determine whether the father's relationship with his child is constitutionally protected because of the procedural protections that result if constitutional rights exist. The Supreme Court has recognized a birth parent's right to direct the upbringing of his or her child as a fundamental liberty interest protected by the Fourteenth Amendment of the United States Constitution.[4] Described as "one of the oldest of the fundamental liberty interests,"[5] the parental right has been applied to protect many parental decisions. For example, it prevents the state from directing a child's religious upbringing,[6] choosing with whom the child should associate,[7] and making medical decisions for the child.[8] These holdings rest on the premise that the "natural bonds of affection lead parents to act in the best interests of their children."[9]

Benefits for Foster Children when Nonresident Fathers are Involved

A multistate study using data supplied by states that participated in the original *What About the Dads* study found that children whose fathers were more involved:

➤ had a higher likelihood of reunification and a lower likelihood of adoption;

➤ were discharged from foster care more quickly than those with less or no paternal involvement; and

➤ had substantially lower likelihood of subsequent maltreatment allegations.

Engaging fathers in their children's lives is also linked to children's:

➤ improved physical and mental health;

➤ improved self-esteem;

➤ responsible sexuality;

➤ emotional maturity; and

➤ greater financial security.

In contrast, children in homes without fathers tend to:

➤ experience high rates of poverty at an earlier age;

➤ have problems in school; and

➤ become involved with the criminal justice system.

Sources:

Malm, K., E. Zielewski and H. Chen. *More about the Dads: Exploring Associations between Nonresident Father Involvement and Child Welfare Case Outcomes*. Washington, D.C.: U.S. Department of Health and Human Services, Office of the Assistant Secretary for Planning and Evaluation, 2008. Available at: http://aspe.hhs.gov/hsp/08/moreaboutdads/index.htm; Horn, W. and T. Sylvester. *Father Facts: Fifth Edition*. Gaithersburg, MD: National Fatherhood Initiative, 2007; National Child Welfare Resource Center for Family-Centered Practice. "Father Involvement in Child Welfare: Estrangement and Reconciliation." *Best Practice/Next Practice: Family Centered Child Welfare,* Summer 2002.

Parents' constitutional rights in child welfare proceedings

In child protection cases, this right has fueled constitutionally-based procedural protections for parents. If the state seeks to remove a child from the home, an emergency hearing must be held promptly and the state must prove why removal is necessary. Before the state assumes extended custody of the child, a finding of unfitness is required. The parent must receive adequate notice and a meaningful opportunity to be heard at the hearing where this finding is made.[10] Before the state terminates parental rights, it must prove parental unfitness by clear and convincing evidence[11] at a hearing. Due process may mandate appointing counsel to represent the parent at this hearing.[12] Thus, resolving this threshold question—whether the nonresident father's relationship with his child is constitutionally-protected—is crucial in determining if he is entitled to other constitutional protections, all of which trump conflicting federal and state statutes.

Federal constitutional rights

How do you determine whether a nonresident father is entitled to constitutional protections?

Parental involvement

The Supreme Court has answered this question by looking at the level of involvement of the nonresident father in his child's life. "When a father demonstrates a full commitment to the responsibilities of parenthood by coming forward to participate in the rearing of his child, his interest in personal contact with his child acquires substantial protection under the Due Process Clause."[13] For example, in *Lehr v. Robertson*, the Supreme Court upheld a New York statute that did not require a father to be notified of his child's impending adoption because the father did not take meaningful steps to establish a parental relationship with his child.[14] The Court reasoned:

> The significance of the biological connection is that it offers the natural father an opportunity that no other male possesses to develop a relationship with his offspring. If he grasps that opportunity and accepts some measure of responsibility for the child's future, he may enjoy the blessings of the parent-child relationship and make uniquely valuable contributions to the child's development. If he fails to do so, the Federal Constitution will not automatically compel a State to listen to his opinion of where the child's best interests lie.[15]

Similarly, in *Quilloin v. Walcott*, the Court held that a birth father, who had minimal contact with the child, could not disrupt a child's adoption into a family with whom the child had already been living.[16] In both decisions, the Supreme Court prevented fathers who had not made efforts to establish a relationship with their children from using the Constitution to disrupt the child's permanent placement.

But when the father has such a relationship, the Court has prevented states from infringing on the father-child bond without providing adequate process. In *Caban v. Mohammed*, the Court struck down a New York statute that denied a father the right to object to an adoption to which the biological mother had

Supreme Court Cases Addressing the Rights of Nonresident Fathers

➤ *Stanley v. Illinois*, 405 U.S. 645 (1972).

➤ *Quilloin v. Walcott*, 434 U.S. 246 (1978).

➤ *Caban v. Mohammed*, 441 U.S. 380 (1979).

➤ *Lehr v. Robertson*, 463 U.S. 248 (1983).

➤ *Michael H. v. Gerald D.*, 491 U.S. 110 (1989).

already consented.[17] The Court held that since the father was as involved in the children's upbringing as their mother, they both had to be treated equally.[18] Although the Supreme Court has never proscribed the specific actions a nonresident father must take to perfect his constitutionally-protected interest in his child, the Court's rulings clarify that the rights of fathers who have established relationships with their children are constitutionally protected from state interference absent proof of unfitness.

Paternity establishment

Additionally, the Supreme Court has held that due process requires states to give all fathers the opportunity to establish parental relationships by allowing them to claim their interest in the child soon after the child's birth.[19] States have created several ways for fathers to assert parentage. In some states, fathers have to file an affidavit of paternity jointly with the child's mother or institute a paternity suit. Others use putative father registries to let fathers assert their interests. State practices vary on this issue; as the father's lawyer, you will need to know these differences. Most appellate courts find a father's failure to comply with state procedures constitutes a permanent waiver of the father's rights to his child.[20]

Exceptions

Extending substantial protections to a birth father who has a relationship with his child and allowing all fathers an opportunity to claim their parental interest soon after the child's birth are well-established principles. The only exception is when, under state law, another man, typically the husband of the child's mother, has been designated the child's legal father. A number of states have strong presumptions that the husband of the child's mother is the legal father if the child was born during the marriage. In these states, even if another man claims to be the

■ Additional Resources

➤ Greene, Angela. "The Crab Fisherman and His Children: A Constitutional Compass for the Non-Offending Parent in Child Protection Cases." *Alaska Law Review* 24, 2007, 173, 181-199.

➤ Harris, Leslie Joan. "Involving Nonresident Fathers in Dependency Cases: New Efforts, New Problems, New Solutions." *Journal of Family Studies* 9, 2007, 281, 307.

➤ Sankaran, Vivek S. "But I Didn't Do Anything Wrong: Revisiting the Rights of Non-Offending Parents in Child Protection Proceedings." *Michigan Bar Journal* 85, March 2006, 22.

child's birth father, he does not have any standing to assert his rights since the law recognizes someone else as the child's legal father. This statutory scheme was challenged in *Michael H. v. Gerald D.*, where the Supreme Court, in a split decision, affirmed these statutes.[21]

Be aware of the intricacies of your state's paternity laws to decide how your clients' rights may be impacted if another man claims to have a parental relationship with the child. For example, some jurisdictions, like Louisiana, have allowed courts to permit dual paternity in limited situations.[22]

➤ Practice tips

How do these constitutional principles translate into good practice? Once the nonresident father is identified, you will need to determine his prior involvement in the child's life.

- Did he pay child support? When, and how frequently?
- How often did he visit the child?
- Did he provide the child's mother any assistance during her pregnancy?
- Did he send gifts and/or cards to the child?
- Did he attend school meetings or take the child to doctor appointments?
- Is his name on the birth certificate?

Answering these questions will flesh out whether the father developed the type of relationship with his child that courts deem constitutionally protected. If a relationship exists, the father is guaranteed the due process protections noted above, regardless of conflicting state and federal laws, unless state law has designated another person as the child's legal father. If no other legal father exists, the father must be given notice and an opportunity to be heard and the state cannot interfere with his custodial rights absent proof of unfitness. His rights to the child are substantial and state encroachment must be justified by compelling reasons.

If a relationship does not exist, assess whether the father's opportunity to establish a parental relationship was blocked in any way.

- Does state law provide adequate mechanisms for the father to become involved in the child's life?
- Did the child's mother in some way prevent the father from developing a relationship with the child?
- Did the father make all reasonable efforts to form a parental relationship?
- Was the child taken into state care almost immediately after birth (e.g., from the hospital)?

If evidence shows the father never had a meaningful opportunity to create a parental bond with his child, you could argue that the Constitution requires that he be given the opportunity. In *Lehr*, the Supreme Court specifically analyzed whether state law protected a father's right to form such a relationship. Evidence of fraud or concealment on the part of the mother or the state agency may help persuade a judge to give the father an opportunity to assert his rights. When representing nonresident fathers, ensure that the constitutional protections given to all parents are afforded to those fathers whose prior actions merit such protection.

Determining if State Law Protects Fathers' Rights

Assuming the nonresident father has perfected his constitutional rights to his child, you must next determine whether provisions under state law are constitutional.

- Does state law provide him with notice and an opportunity to be heard about his child's custody?
- Does it give him a presumption of parental fitness?

If not, the state may have impermissibly encroached upon his rights based solely on a subjective determination of what is best for his child. Thoroughly understanding the interplay between constitutional rights and state statutory provisions is crucial in vindicating the rights of nonresident fathers.

◼ Tips for Agency Lawyers

Child welfare agency lawyers also have an important role to play in ensuring that fathers' constitutional rights are protected. You can take the following steps:

➤ Ensure the nonresident father is identified and located early in the case and receives notice of all child protective proceedings.

➤ Ensure the child welfare agency conducts comprehensive assessments of nonresident fathers (and any paternal relatives who express interest) immediately after they request custody or visitation.

➤ Encourage caseworkers to include the father in his child's case plan, focus on his strengths, and offer him appropriate services.

➤ If no evidence of parental unfitness exists, counsel the child welfare agency that the father has a constitutional right to obtain custody over his child.

➤ Ensure court orders and agency practices do not hinder the father's right to visit with his child without proof that it may harm or endanger the child's safety or well-being.

➤ Remember that all parties in child welfare proceedings need to work together to ensure that constitutional rights are respected, delays and appeals are minimized and reunification or other permanency outcomes are achieved promptly.

Generally, most states provide nonresident fathers basic procedural rights to:
- notice of proceedings and opportunity to participate;
- visitation with children; and
- court-appointed counsel if indigent.

But states vary considerably on two key issues: 1) whether the child must be placed with the nonresident father absent proof of unfitness, and 2) whether the court can order a fit nonresident father to comply with services it deems are in the child's best interests. Differing state approaches to these issues are described below.

No parental presumption

A number of states, such as Michigan and Ohio, have policies permitting courts to deprive nonresident fathers of custodial rights to their children immediately upon an adjudication or plea finding that the mother abused or neglected them.[23] In these jurisdictions, immediately upon a finding against one parent, the trial court obtains custody of the child and can issue any order it deems is in the child's best interest. Even absent a finding of unfitness against the nonresident father, the court can place the child in foster care, compel the nonresident father to comply with services, and order that the father's rights be terminated based on failure to comply with those services. These systems treat nonresident fathers as legal strangers to the child, and the burden is on them to prove to the court it is in the child's best interest to be placed with them.

Deprivation of legal custody

Other jurisdictions have adopted a more nuanced approach while continuing to deprive nonresident fathers of full custodial rights.[24] In these courts, judges recognize the constitutionally-based parental presumption but only apply the presumption to the physical custody of the child. Absent a finding of unfitness, nonresident fathers are granted physical custody of their children, but the court still retains legal custody. That is, the court makes decisions about the child and can order the nonresident father to comply with services. While safeguarding the physical custody rights of nonoffending parents, these systems restrict their legal custody.

No jurisdiction

Finally, two states, Maryland and Pennsylvania, have adopted a completely different approach.[25] In those states, if a nonresident father is willing to immediately assume care and custody of the child and is not unfit, the court may not assume jurisdiction over the child for any purpose, even to offer services to the offending parent or the child. The juvenile court must dismiss the case and the only limited action it may take is to grant custody to the nonresident father before dismissal. Once the custody transfer is made, all court involvement or oversight will end.

As the brief discussion above shows, states differ significantly on whether the nonresident father has a presumptive right to custody of his child and whether he can be forced to comply with services.[26] If a state's practices conflict with the procedural protections guaranteed by the Constitution, it is essential to file all necessary pleadings to safeguard such rights. These may include:
- making a request at the detention or shelter care hearing for immediate placement of the child with the father;
- filing a motion challenging the imposition of services on your client absent a finding of unfitness; and
- arguing that if a fit nonresident father requests custody, then the court cannot interfere with his custodial rights in any way.

Appeals of trial court decisions should be taken immediately, as opposed to waiting until after the father's rights are terminated because, at that point, many of the challenges may be moot or be deemed waived by the court. Of course, the specific arguments that you should make in a given case will depend on the wishes and interests of the client. Always remember to evaluate whether the decisions made by the court and the child welfare agency protect fathers' constitutional rights.

Conclusion

Traditionally, the basic constitutional rights of nonresident fathers in child welfare cases have been given short shrift. As an advocate for nonresident fathers, you can change this dynamic by challenging practices that violate the basic procedural protections that the Constitution provides many fathers. By doing so, the child protection system will begin opening its doors more widely to invite fathers to actively plan for their children's well-being.

Endnotes

1. For a comprehensive study of paternal involvement in child welfare cases, *see* Sonenstein, F., K. Malm and A. Billing. *Study of Fathers' Involvement in Permanency Planning and Child Welfare Casework*. Washington, D.C.: U.S. Department of Health and Human Services, Office of the Assistant Secretary for Planning and Evaluation, 2002. <http://aspe.hhs.gov/hsp/CW-dads02>

2. *See* Malm K., J. Murray and R. Geen. *What about the Dads? Child Welfare Agencies' Efforts to Identify, Locate and Involve Nonresident Fathers*. Washington, D.C.: U.S. Department of Health and Human Services, Office of the Assistant Secretary for Planning and Evaluation, 2006, which explores the reasons why child welfare agencies have traditionally excluded fathers from the case-planning process. <http://aspe.hhs.gov/hsp/06/CW-involve-dads/index.htm>

3. For an analysis of the ways that paternal involvement in child welfare cases enhances child well-being, *see* Malm, K., E. Zielewski and H. Chen. *More about the Dads: Exploring Associations between Nonresident Father Involvement and Child Welfare Case Outcomes*. Washington, D.C.: U.S. Department of Health and Human Services, Office of the Assistant Secretary for Planning and Evaluation, 2008. <http://aspe.hhs.gov/hsp/08/moreaboutdads/index.htm>

4. Meyer v. Nebraska, 262 U.S. 390 (1923).

5. Troxel v. Granville, 450 U.S. 57, 65 (2000).

6. Wisconsin v. Yoder, 406 U.S. 205 (1972).

7. Troxel, 450 U.S. at 57.

8. Parham v. J.R., 442 U.S. 584, 603 (1979).

9. Ibid., 603.

10. Stanley v. Illinois, 405 U.S. 645 (1972).

11. Santosky v. Kramer, 455 U.S. 745 (1982).

12. Lassiter v. Dep't of Social Services, 452 U.S. 18 (1981).

13. Lehr v. Roberstson, 463 U.S. 248, 261 (1983).

14. Ibid., 248.

15. Ibid., 262.

16. Quilloin v. Walcott, 434 U.S. 246, 255 (1977).

17. Caban v. Mohammed, 441 U.S. 380 (1979).

18. Ibid., 389.

19. Lehr, 463 U.S. at 262-263.

20. *See*, *e.g.*, Marco C. v. Sean C., 181 P.3d 1137 (Az. Ct. App. 2008); Heidbreder v. Carton, 645 N.W.2d 355 (Minn. 2002); Hylland v. Doe, 867 P.2d 551 (Or. Ct. App. 1994); Sanchez v. L.D.S. Social Services, 680 P.2d 753 (Utah 1984) (all refusing to permit fathers to assert parental rights where they did not comply with statutory requirements).

21. Michael H. v. Gerald D., 491 U.S. 110 (1989).

22. Smith v. Cole, 553 So. 2d 847 (La. 1989).

23. For Ohio cases, *see*, *e.g.*, In re C.R., 843 N.E.2d 1188 (Ohio 2006); In re Russel, 2006 Ohio App. LEXIS 6565 (Ohio Ct. App. 2006); In re Osberry, 2003 Ohio App. LEXIS 4922 (Ohio Ct. App. 2003). Michigan's approach is exemplified in the following cases: In re Church, 2006 Mich. App. LEXIS 1098 (Mich. Ct. App. 2006); In re Camp, 2006 Mich. App. LEXIS 1620 (Mich. Ct. App. 2006); In re Stramaglia, 2005 Mich. App. LEXIS 1339 (Mich. Ct. App. 2005).

24. *See*, *e.g.*, J.P. v. Dep't of Children and Families, 855 So. 2d 175 (Fla. Dist. Ct. App. 2003); In re Jeffrey P., 218 Cal. App. 3d 1548 (Ct. App. 1990).

25. *See*, *e.g.*, In re M.L., 757 A.2d 849 (Pa. 2000); In re Russell G., 672 A.2d 109 (Md. Ct. Spec. App. 1996).

26. None of these states specifically distinguish between mothers and fathers. However, in practice, these different approaches typically affect the noncustodial parents who most often are fathers.

CHAPTER TWO

Understanding Male Help-Seeking Behaviors

Mark S. Kiselica

CHECKLIST

Understanding Male Help-Seeking Behaviors

Recognize your father client's life circumstances, perform outreach, and remove barriers to his meeting with you.

➤ Consult his caseworker about transportation vouchers or driving services.

➤ Look into additional services, such as job placement and substance abuse counseling (through the agency or in the community).

➤ Explain how criminal charges, immigration status, and child support payments may affect the case. Help alleviate any fears the father may have about getting involved because of these issues.

Explain your role in the child welfare system and who you represent.

➤ Explain to the father that you will advocate for him to your fullest ability.

➤ Assure him that you do not work for anyone else but him.

➤ Explain that anything he tells you is confidential (discuss any relevant exceptions).

Use the strengths of traditional masculinity, while addressing self-defeating beliefs about getting help.

➤ Discuss with the father his beliefs about what it means to be a good man and father.

➤ Help him understand how a father's absence affects a child's life and the positive impact when a father is present and involved with his child.

Address any negative biases you might have about fathers.

➤ Be open minded and positive with each new father you meet.

Learn and practice male-friendly rapport-building tactics.

➤ Greet your client with a firm handshake and sit side-by-side rather than face-to-face.

➤ Share a little bit about your own life and background.

➤ Discuss important events in his community.

Download this and other checklists at **www.fatherhoodqic.org/checklists**

A s a lawyer or judge interacting with nonresident fathers in the child welfare system, you have an opportunity to help fathers play a meaningful role in their children's lives. This may involve helping fathers obtain and use services offered to them by child welfare caseworkers and other family service providers.[1] Some fathers may need help to be more trusting and open toward the legal and child welfare systems. Others will need to be encouraged to show interest in and have contact with their children and the professionals who serve them.

This chapter discusses several factors that influence help-seeking behavior and service use by fathers. Understanding these factors and behaviors can help you discover fathers' strengths and recognize how they can be important assets in the lives of their children. Many fathers want to be a part of their children's lives and can be helped to do so through your advocacy and support.

Addressing Barriers to Male Engagement

The following discussion explores common barriers to child welfare system involvement and help-seeking by men and offers strategies to address them. Many of these tips relate to fostering a strong lawyer-client relationship, but they also are about how the system can and should respond to fathers. It is part of the lawyer's role to inform the child welfare system of these issues so that courts and agencies can better interact with fathers.

Individual barriers

Stressful life circumstances and practical barriers

Nonresident fathers are likely to be poor and struggling to survive tough life circumstances. Compared to fathers who reside with their children, nonresident fathers tend to:

- have greater financial problems;
- move more often;
- have more children;
- have greater difficulty finding child care;
- experience more emotional problems; and
- have higher rates of drug and alcohol abuse, antisocial behavior, domestic violence, homelessness, and unemployment.[2]

About 40% of nonresident fathers involved in the child welfare system have four or more of these hardships.[3] Responding to these problems can be so consuming that many fathers are too overwhelmed to participate on behalf of their children, even when they would prefer to be involved.

Numerous practical barriers prevent fathers from getting involved with the child welfare system. Some are linked to institutional practices and others to the life circumstances discussed above. Most agencies and institutions associated with the child welfare system are open only during daylight hours on weekdays. For many fathers, these hours conflict with their work schedules, which are not negotiable. Getting to and from a child welfare office or court is an unpredictable endeavor for fathers who lack reliable transportation. Others cannot travel because they are incarcerated.[4] Some don't even know they are fathers or the child's mother prevents them from establishing a relationship with the child. These barriers prevent many fathers from having any say in proceedings about their children.

> "A lot of these guys come in and they have no idea how the system works. They have just come out of prison and haven't seen their kids in years, you know? So they're like completely in a fog about where to go, the certain connections you need to make, or the paperwork to file a motion. At the same time, they don't really have a lot of hope. And people who don't really have a lot of hope have a hard time following through."
>
> —*Fatherhood program director*

➤ Practice tips

Recognize the father's life circumstances, perform outreach, and remove practical barriers.

- Because nonresident fathers struggle with many hardships, they may arrive late for appointments and miss some appointments altogether. Missing meetings does not necessarily mean that the father doesn't want help. Be patient and persistent.
- Call the father during non-work hours to discuss his difficulties in making meetings.
- Pay attention to any concerns he might want to discuss, not just those pertaining to legal proceedings, and then through interprofessional collaboration assist him with any problem he might have.
- Consult his caseworker to see if assistance can be arranged, such as transportation vouchers or volunteer driving services.
- Ask your superiors about staffing your office on some evenings and weekends so your availability is not limited to times the father must work.

- Explain to the father that you can help him access services that he may need by consulting with his caseworker.
- With the father's permission, inform the caseworker about any nonlegal problems he might have, and ask if additional services, such as job placement and substance abuse counseling, can be provided when they are warranted.[5]

Fear of prosecution

Many fathers believe contact with the child welfare system will get them in trouble with the law. Fathers who are behind in their child support payments are often hesitant to advocate for their children, fearing that participating in child welfare proceedings will result in their being identified for arrearages that they may be unable to pay because they are destitute.[6] (See Chapter 7, *Using Legal Strategies to Address Child Support Obligations*.) Some fathers avoid child welfare officials because they are undocumented immigrants concerned about possible deportation. Fathers with substance abuse histories worry that they could face criminal penalties associated with their illegal use and distribution of drugs.[7] Adult fathers whose former partners are still minors could be charged with statutory rape.[8] Fathers with criminal histories who have committed no new crimes may have little trust of the legal system. Ex-offenders also may avoid professionals who ask too many questions because they associate frequent questioning with being interrogated by police investigators, prosecutors, and prison officials.[9] Thus, fear of prosecution and the lingering effects of prior criminal justice system involvement can cause fathers to be guarded when dealing with the child welfare system. (See Chapter 6, *Addressing Special Advocacy Issues*.)

➤ Practice tips

Explain your role in the child welfare system and who you represent.

- After you have established a rapport with the father, assure him that you do not work for his child's mother because he may have a conflicted, adversarial relationship with her.[10]
- Explain the child welfare system and your role in it, being careful not to overwhelm him with too much information. It can help to give him a diagram depicting the various components in the system and your role in it.
- Use simple language rather than technical terms or "legalese" while describing the child welfare system.[11]
- Assure the father you are not there to prosecute him for any current

The *Father Friendly Check-Up*™ for Child Welfare Agencies and Organizations

The National Fatherhood Initiative's *Father Friendly Check-Up*™ helps organizations assess how well they welcome and encourage fathers in several areas—leadership, organizational philosophy, policies and procedures, programs, physical environment, staff orientation and training, social marketing strategies, and service to the community.

As part of the Quality Improvement Center on Non-Resident Fathers and the Child Welfare System, the National Fatherhood Initiative developed a version of the *Father Friendly Check-Up* specifically for child welfare agencies and organizations. This tool, available at www.fatherhoodqic.org, can help you understand what efforts the agency could be making for fathers, and spark ideas for changes you can make in your practice. For example, use the tool to find out whether your organization:

➤ expects staff to include a father component in new staff orientation and training activities;

➤ encourages fathers/men in their cases to balance work and family life;

➤ expects staff to avoid using language that is divisive and that stereotypes men/fathers and women/mothers;

➤ has family restrooms or a diaper deck in the men's restroom;

➤ has staff who have been trained to work with fathers in a gender-responsive, nonaccusatory, nonblaming manner;

➤ maintains lists of recommended resources for fathers (e.g., fatherhood classes and support groups).

Source:

National Fatherhood Initiative. *Father Friendly Check-Up*™ *for Child Welfare Agencies and Organizations*, available at www.fatherhoodqic.org.

or former offenses, and inform him about the limits of confidentiality. Give him plenty of time to absorb and react to this information.

• Empathize with and address fears he might have about his involvement with you, and respond to all of his questions, as well as any angry comments, in a concerned and nondefensive manner (e.g., don't take it personally if the father says that working with you is a waste of time because the system is unfair to fathers).

• Express your empathy for his distrust of the system, and assure him that you are going to do everything in your power to assist him. The most important message you can give him during this phase is that you will advocate for him to your fullest ability and you want to help him with his most pressing concerns and needs.[12]

- Ask him about his own family as a potential placement option for his child or children, which conveys to him your advocacy for his extended family.[13] Taking these measures will help dispel misconceptions he might have about child welfare proceedings, while allaying mistrust he might have about you.

Traditional notions of masculinity

The cultural demands of masculinity deter men who adhere to traditional gender roles from seeking help. Many tasks associated with help seeking, such as relying on others, admitting that one needs help, and presenting oneself as vulnerable, conflict with traditional concepts of what it means to be a man.[14] Research links traditional male beliefs in men with their negative attitudes about getting assistance from others.[15] Men who live up to cultural expectations by remaining stoic, completely self-reliant, and unbending in the face of adversity harm themselves through their decisions not to seek help when they are ill, in mental distress, or need crucial information that could enhance their lives. Yet men who fail to meet these expectations risk being judged harshly by other traditional men.[16] Thus, fathers who come from a more traditional orientation resist turning to child welfare professionals for help, even though they may be in considerable distress about the situation with their children.

➤ Practice tips

Use the strengths of traditional masculinity, while addressing self-defeating beliefs about getting help.

- Discuss the father's beliefs about what it means to be a good man and father.
- Affirm those aspects of traditional masculinity that will enhance his performance as a father, such as his desire to protect his children, and his willingness to work hard, for long hours, and in difficult conditions to be a good provider.
- Point out that it takes guts to seek and accept help, and that it takes courage to deal with the child welfare system.
- Point out that every man needs help from time to time, and that you can help "cover his back" as he works with the system.
- Explore with him the problems that can occur if he decides to go it alone or to attack the system in an overly macho fashion.

- If he is a very traditional male, he is likely to set aside his strong need to address his problems on his own if he feels he is part of a team because traditional men are used to forming friendships and completing tasks in groups. Invite him to form a team with you, suggesting that the two of you will tackle the issues that arise in his case together.[17]
- Explore with him his hopes and dreams for his children, and then explain how you can help him devise a plan for working with the child welfare system to help make those hopes and dreams a reality.[18]

Institutional and professional barriers

Institutional practices

For over a century, the child welfare system has been guided by the belief that mothers are crucial to child development, especially during a child's early years.[19] Until recently, fathers were deemed relatively unimportant except for their ability to provide economic support for their wives or partners and their children.[20] Consequently, child welfare professionals have focused on repairing and restoring mother-child relationships, while viewing fathers only in terms of their duties as providers of child support. Faced with this bias, fathers are understandably skeptical that the child welfare system will consider their interests. Like most people, fathers have great difficulty trusting and participating in systems in which they don't feel valued.

➤ Practice tips

Request in-service workshops on fathers that promote awareness, knowledge, and skills.

- Encourage child welfare and court administrators to provide training about fathers and their needs. Workshops should cover: a) awareness-raising activities designed to help professionals examine their biases about fathers and explore how any personal issues with men might affect their work with fathers; b) information about the characteristics, hardships, and needs of fathers; and c) education about how to help fathers in a male-friendly manner.
- Since ethnic-minority populations are overrepresented among fathers whose children are in the child welfare system, diversity training is an essential part of continuing education workshops.

Advocate for father-supportive policies.

- Support or promote legislative or policy reforms that increase involvement of fathers in child welfare cases. These may include:

- **Right to counsel:** The right of fathers to court-appointed counsel should be expanded. It is important that fathers also receive legal assistance regarding child custody, visitation, and support issues that are interconnected with their participating in the child welfare proceeding.[21]

- **Funding for father-service programs:** Society benefits from public policies that fund father-service programs that prepare and support fathers with their parenting duties and address any personal problems—homelessness, substance abuse, and re-entry into society after imprisonment—that prevent them from parenting successfully.[22]

- **Child support reform:** Because child welfare fathers tend to be poor, they often have trouble paying child support. Child support enforcement policies must be flexible and geared toward a man's ability to pay, while providing him credit for other factors, such as number of contacts with his child, participation in parenting classes, enrollment and attendance in GED, college, and vocational education courses, and provision of in-kind support.[23] Another innovative policy change is linking child-support enforcement with workforce development, which would help more fathers become self-sufficient parents.[24] Child support obligations for fathers in prison should be frozen or reduced to cover only nominal wages earned while in prison.[25]

- **Welfare reform:** "Pass-through" policies permit formal child support by low-income fathers to pass through to their families instead of being collected by the state to recoup the costs of public assistance paid to the custodial mother.[26] Implementing pass-through policies will likely increase the number of fathers declaring paternity and participating in the child support system, while fostering a standard of living that allows low-income fathers to meet their basic needs.

Pejorative stereotypes

Distrust of the child welfare system is also fueled by pejorative biases many professionals have about fathers. Stereotypes about fathers within this system are abundant. Fathers are often viewed by child welfare professionals as a threat, a liability, potentially violent even when they have no history of violence, potentially abusive toward children, uncooperative, recalcitrant, unable to take responsibility, and uncommitted to family life.[27] Although these characterizations are accurate for some, many want to be stable, loving fathers for their children. Fathers who sense these derogatory attitudes about them during their initial encounters with the child welfare system are unlikely to cooperate.

➤ Practice tips

Address any negative biases about fathers.

- Recognize that fathers are complex. Although some fit the stereotype of the man who is unconcerned about his children, many others care deeply about their children's well-being and have the capacity to be outstanding fathers.
- Maintain an open mind and a positive perspective with each new father you meet.
- Look for and affirm fathers who want to be a constructive presence in their children's lives.[28]

Female orientation of the child welfare system

Fathers can feel uncomfortable in the child welfare environment because of its strong female orientation. Over 80% of the caseworkers employed in the child welfare system are women.[29] These professionals, though dedicated and well intentioned, are sometimes uneasy or afraid to work with fathers. Many female caseworkers can empathize with their women clients, but have difficulty relating to fathers, especially those who are hostile and angry toward the system.

Some caseworkers use rapport building and interventions that work well with women but not men. For example, although sitting face to face, asking open-ended questions, and focusing discussions to disclose emotions tend to be effective with women clients, they are ill-suited for work with many men. Males who adhere to traditional notions of masculinity prefer side-by-side conversations focused on information- and advice-giving and active problem-solving.[30] Due to the strong female orientation of the child welfare system, fathers may feel the entire system lacks a male perspective on how to approach and resolve problems.

➤ Practice tips

Learn and practice male-friendly rapport-building tactics.

- Although your work with fathers involves serious legal matters, try to make your early conversations warm, friendly, and informal.
- If possible, have all phone calls held until your session with the father is over, which lets you give him your undivided attention while communicating that his concerns are your priority.
- Greet him with a firm handshake and a reassuring smile.
- Offer him a soft drink or a snack to help him relax.
- Sit or take a walk with him side-by-side, rather than face-to-face, as you get to know him.

- Share a little bit about your own life and background.
- Ask him about his work and interests and respond positively.
- Be knowledgeable about and prepared to discuss important events in his community.
- If appropriate, use slang that is common in the community, and ask him to explain any local expressions you might not understand.
- Try infusing a joke into your conversations with him from time to time, which is a common tactic men use with each other to diffuse tension[31] (e.g., make a humorous, self-deprecating comment about yourself or engage him in some good-natured ribbing to loosen him up).

Conclusion

For most men, being a loving, competent father is one of their most important roles. Many barriers prevent nonresident fathers whose children have been placed in the child welfare system from fulfilling this role. Legal professionals who understand the complicated hardships of these men, engage them in a male-friendly way, and advocate on their behalf are likely to help them be responsible, caring participants in their children's lives. When that is not possible, these strategies can also help to identify the father's extended family members, who could play a meaningful role for the child in the father's absence.

The author thanks his colleagues at the American Bar Association, the National Fatherhood Initiative, American Humane, and the Children's Bureau for their helpful feedback on drafts of this chapter.

Endnotes

1. Other service providers may include local job placement programs, fatherhood programs, and GED programs. Malm, K., J. Murray and R. Geen. *What about the Dads? Child Welfare Agencies' Efforts to Identify, Locate and Involve Nonresident Fathers*. Washington, D.C.: U.S. Department of Health and Human Services, Office of the Assistant Secretary for Planning and Evaluation, 2006.

2. Ibid.; *see also* Jaffe, S., et al. "Predicting Early Fatherhood and Whether Young Fathers Live with Their Children: Prospective Findings and Policy Reconsiderations." *Journal of Child Psychology, Psychiatry and Allied Disciplines* 42, 2001, 803-815.

3. Malm et al., 2006.

4. Ibid.

5. Kiselica, Mark. *When Boys Become Parents: Adolescent Fatherhood in America*. New Brunswick, NJ: Rutgers University Press, 2008.

6. National Family Preservation Network. "An Assessment of Child Welfare Practices Regarding Fathers." Prepared for the Annie E. Casey Foundation, 2001. Retrieved online on September 5, 2008 at www.nfpn.org/tools—training/articles/an-assessment-of-child-welfare-practices-regarding-fathers.html.

7. Malm et al., 2006.

8. Kiselica, 2008.

9. Ibid.

10. Malm et al., 2006.

11. Morley, Lauren, Leslie Wilmot, Jane Berdie, Lara Bruce and Paul Frankel. *Bringing Back the Dads: A Model Program Curriculum for Non-Resident Father Engagement.* Englewood, CO: American Humane Association, 2008.

12. Kiselica, 2008.

13. Malm et al., 2006.

14. Englar-Carlson, Matt. "Masculine Norms and the Therapy Process." In *In the Room with Men: A Casebook of Therapeutic Change,* by Matt Englar-Carlson and Mark Stevens. Washington, D.C.: American Psychological Association, 2006.

15. Mahalik, James R., Glenn E. Good and Matt Englar-Carlson. "Masculinity Scripts, Presenting Concerns, and Help Seeking: Implications for Practice and Training." *Professional Psychology: Research and Practice* 34(2), 2003, 123-131.

16. Englar-Carlson, 2006.

17. Kiselica, Mark, Matt Englar-Carlson, Arthur M. Horne and Mark Fisher. "A Positive Psychology Perspective on Helping Boys." In *Counseling Troubled Boys: A Guidebook for Professionals*, by Mark Kiselica, Matt Englar-Carlson and Arthur Horne. New York: Routledge, 2008.

18. Kiselica, 2008.

19. Jaffe, Eliezer D. "Fathers and Child Welfare Services: The Forgotten Clients." In *Fatherhood and Social Policy*, by Michael E. Lamb and Abraham Sagi. Hillsdale, NJ: Erlbaum, 1983.

20. National Academy of Sciences. *America's Fathers and Public Policy: Introduction*, 1994. Retrieved online on May 4, 2007 at http://books.nap.edu/html/amerfath/chapter1.html.

21. Kiselica, 2008.

22. Ibid.

23. Pirog-Good, M.A. and D.H. Good. *Child Support Enforcement for Teenage Fathers: Problems and Prospects*. Discussion Paper no. 1029-94, Madison, WI: Institute for Research on Poverty, University of Wisconsin, 1994. Retrieved online on April 30, 2007 at http://ideas.repec.org/p/wop/wispod/1029-94.html.

24. Miller, C. and V. Knox. *The Challenge of Helping Low-Income Fathers Support Their Children: Final Lessons from Parents' Fair Share*. New York: Manpower Research Development, 2001.

25. Wolf, W.C. and S. Leiderman. *Investing in "Young Families:" Some Thoughts on Advantages, Disadvantages and Possible Next Steps*. Trenton, NJ: Center for Assessment and Policy Development, 2001. Available online at www.capd.org/pubfiles/pub-2001-03-02.pdf.

26. Romo, C., J. Bellamy and M.T. Coleman. *TFF Final Evaluation Report*. Austin, TX: Texas Fragile Families Initiative, 2004.

27. Featherstone, H. "Taking Fathers Seriously." *British Journal of Social Work* 33, 2003, 239-254; Greif, J. and C. Bailey. "Where are the Fathers in Social Work Literature?" *Families in Society* 71(2), 1990, 88-92; Marshall, D., D. English and A. Stewart. "The Effect of Fathers or Father Figures on Child Behavioral Problems in Families Referred to Child Protective Services." *Child Maltreatment* 6(4), 2001, 290-299; O'Donnell, J.M., W.E. Johnson Jr., L.E. D'Aunno and H.L. Thornton. "Fathers in Child Welfare: Caseworkers' Perspectives." *Child Welfare* 84(3), 2005, 387–414; Schmid, J. "The Business of Engaging Fathers (and Other Male Relatives) in the FGC Process." *Protecting Children* 21(1), 2006, 20-30.

28. Kiselica, 2008.

29. Malm et al., 2006.

30. Kiselica, 2008.

31. Ibid.; *see also* Leo Hendricks. "Outreach with Teenage Fathers: A Preliminary Report on Three Ethnic Groups." *Adolescence* 23, 1988, 711-720.

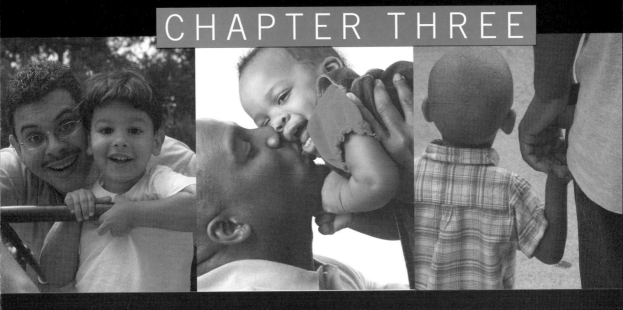

CHAPTER THREE

Ensuring Quality Out-of-Court Advocacy

**Richard Cozzola and
Andrya L. Soprych**

CHECKLIST

Ensuring Quality Out-of-Court Advocacy

Develop a good working attorney-client relationship with your father client.

➤ Explain your role in helping him achieve his goals for his child and discuss that he can confide in you.

➤ Learn about his family, support system, current relationships, and his understanding of the child welfare system, possibly using a genogram.

➤ Discuss his responsibilities and help him understand how his actions influence case outcomes.

Establish an open line of communication with the caseworker.

➤ Find out how the agency views your client, influence the caseworker through education and advocacy, and use the relationship as an opportunity to show your client understands his child's needs.

➤ Use the expertise of social workers in your office to communicate your client's position and needs to the caseworker.

➤ Do not assume the caseworker is an expert on the issues your client faces. You may have to educate yourself and the social worker on your client's needs relating to substance abuse, mental health, criminal system involvement, etc.

➤ Share positive stories with the worker about your client's interaction with his child.

Participate and prepare for child welfare staffings.

➤ Review with your client before the staffing what should or should not be shared.

➤ Translate acronyms or lingo to your client so he understands what is happening.

➤ Explain to your client who will attend the staffing and each person's role.

➤ Be firm when necessary to get needed assistance and to save your client from appearing negative.

➤ If permitted, encourage your client to bring supportive relatives to the staffing.

Download this and other checklists at **www.fatherhoodqic.org/checklists**

When representing nonresident fathers in child welfare cases, your out-of-court advocacy is central to overcoming the challenges your clients face. The challenges may seem obvious. Caseworkers, guardians ad litem, and judges may question the commitment or parenting ability of a father who has not been a significant caretaker for a child. They may also wonder about his involvement in or knowledge of the abuse or neglect that brought the case to court. However, because child welfare proceedings have a goal of finding a safe, permanent home for the child, they provide fathers opportunities to overcome these and other challenges. When a father shows he can play a positive role in the child's life, it increases the chances that the court may place the child with him or a family member.

You can help your client play a positive role in his child's life through three important steps:

- helping him understand the importance of his out-of-court actions;
- working with him and other professionals to allow him to take the positive steps that show his commitment and parenting ability; and
- bringing his progress to the attention of the court.

This chapter explores how your out-of-court advocacy can accomplish these three steps and help achieve your client's goals. By developing a strong lawyer-client relationship, working collaboratively with the agency caseworker, and taking an active role at child welfare meetings and staffings, you will strengthen your advocacy for your father clients.

The Lawyer-Client Relationship

The first step to successfully representing nonresident fathers in child welfare cases is developing a solid lawyer-client relationship. Begin this relationship by helping the father understand how you, as a lawyer, can help him achieve his goals for his child. This means explaining your role and helping the father clarify his goals. Remember that prior to meeting with you, the father may have talked to caseworkers or others during the investigation of a case. Those conversations may have added to his mistrust of people involved with the child welfare system, especially if a caseworker either misunderstood him or used his statements against him. Because of this, your explanation of lawyer-client confidentiality and its limits is crucial. The father needs to know he can confide in you. This also means you and he need to agree on the circumstances when you will communicate his concerns directly to the caseworker and others, and when you will check with him before making such statements.

Once the father understands the basics of confidentiality, your next step is counseling him on his options and strategies for obtaining his goals. Start this process by developing a basic rapport and getting to know him. A first step in developing this rapport is learning about his family, support system, current relationships, and his understanding of the child welfare and juvenile court systems. Learning this information will also help you begin to understand important factors that will impact the case.

One way to learn many of these things is to work with the father to develop a family tree of his parents, siblings, extended family, children, and significant relationships (a genogram[1]). This diagram gives you a quick resource for understanding the people who may become involved in a case and opens the door, in a nonthreatening way, to discuss family members who can provide support, placement resources, or examples of positive relationships. It can also help the father understand the difference between nonrelative foster care and kinship care, as well as other issues he will face in court. (See *Genogram* box.)

Setting goals and responsibilities

When establishing a lawyer-client relationship, work with the father to set goals and accept responsibilities. Ask questions and give him information to help him define his goals in the case. For example:

- Does he want the child to be placed with him?
- Does he believe return home to the mother is a good idea and, if so, what type of involvement does he want in the child's life?
- Does he know he can ask that the child be placed with a family member?[2]
  - Which family member would he prefer?
  - Are there family members with whom the child has an especially positive relationship?[3]

Discuss what he may have to do to accomplish these goals and explain how you can help him meet them.

When setting goals, remember the goals are not static and you will need to revisit and clarify them often. At a minimum, this should occur at all potential case-changing events. For example, one nonresident father, Aaron (see *Genogram* box), began with a goal that his father (the children's grandfather) obtain custody of his three sons. He was concerned about his long-term health and knew the children's mother had repeatedly failed to recover from substance abuse. As the case went on, however, his health stabilized, he got a job, and he gained confidence in his ability to raise his children. One year after reaching his initial goal

Genogram

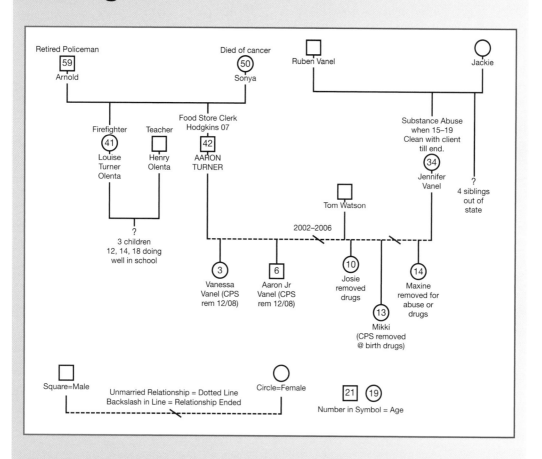

A genogram depicts families and relationships (past and present). It is beyond the scope of this chapter to fully explain how to read a genogram, but once you understand the basic representations, it becomes a valuable tool summarizing pages of information into a one-page chart.[1]

The genogram above represents Aaron Turner, his children, and some of his extended family. It includes the two children he had with Jennifer who are the subject of the juvenile court case. It also includes his parents and sibling, as well as Jennifer's other three children, who have a different father. A more complete genogram would include more extended family and the children's foster placements. Even in this limited scope, it shows several things:

➤ If Aaron cannot care for his children, at least two relatives are placement possibilities.

➤ His father and sibling appear to lead stable lives.

➤ The only children of the mother (Jennifer Vanel) who did not immediately enter the child welfare system were the ones born while she and Aaron were together—demonstrating that he appears to have had a positive impact on the lives of the children he raised even when the mother had a history of substance abuse.

The genogram provides an opening to discuss these issues. At a more detailed level, it outlines the beginnings of a theory of why the children belong in the care of Aaron's family.

Source:

1. McGoldrick, M., R. Gerson and S. Shellenberger. *Genograms: Assessment and Intervention,* 2d ed. New York: Norton, 1999. Special software, such as GenoPro (www.genopro.com), is available to create genograms and store them electronically.

of a placement change to his father, he established a new one—placement of the children with him. An ongoing dialogue between Aaron and his lawyer reinforced that his goal could change as the case evolved, and opened the door to Aaron discussing his changing view of his role in the life of his children.

It is also critical to address the father's responsibilities in the initial interview and reinforce them throughout the case. His responsibilities include those he must take to achieve his goals and his responsibilities to you. He may believe legal work alone can "save" his case. However, it is impossible to help a father gain custody of a child unless he shows his caretaking ability and concern for the child.[4] Even if the father's goal is to have the child placed with someone else, he will still need to participate in the case and services to have his voice heard. If your client understands that he can influence the case through his involvement, it can become a source of power and control for him. Help him maintain his sense of responsibility by letting him know that while you may occasionally take the lead talking to agency workers, and mental health treatment and other service providers, his actions are far more important in determining his future role. His interactions with child welfare professionals and his decisions, actions, reactions, or lack of action will greatly affect the case outcome.

Revisit the issue of responsibility repeatedly. One technique is to remind the client of your respective roles as team members seeking to accomplish his goals. When he participates in visitation or other services, use your skills as his lawyer to let the judge know about his progress. On the other hand if he does not follow through in his responsibilities, you have no positive evidence to give the court. ("John, what are you doing this week that we'll be able to tell the judge about next month?")

Finally, discuss when he should contact you. At a minimum, ask him to agree to contact you when he learns of upcoming meetings with caseworkers or when he has a concern about an event. Make sure he understands he can and should call you with questions about issues such as visitation and services. Explain that in your role as lawyer it is important for you to know when he has made a mistake, such as missing a visit, or when he runs into an obstacle such as a scheduling conflict. Make sure he understands that if you know about these issues, you can then work together to resolve them, and that in-court surprises are never helpful. This is also a good time to re-discuss how lawyer-client confidentiality applies to these situations.

Communicating with the Caseworker

While the lawyer-client relationship provides the foundation for representation, the next element in out-of-court advocacy, working with the social service staff, is just as critical. The court relies on the caseworkers, supervisors, and service providers to learn whether the father has progressed towards his goals. (See *Tips for Working with Service Providers* box.) Because of this, you will also have to establish a working relationship with the primary caseworker, even during the early stages of the lawyer-client relationship. The primary workers and their supervisors greatly influence the direction a case goes and the services parents and children receive. Some judges call them the court's "eyes and ears." As the lawyer for the nonresident father, informal advocacy with the worker is crucial to your case.

Gathering information

The caseworker can be a wealth of information for you and your client. A good working relationship allows you to obtain information about the father's progress, learn how the agency views him, and influence the agency's position through education and advocacy.

When you accept a nonresident father as a client, contact the caseworker immediately—before you call with questions, complaints, or any other agenda. This can happen by phone or in the hall outside the courtroom on your first appearance in the case. Introduce yourself and ask if the caseworker has any information she thinks you should know. Let the caseworker know you will be in touch regularly and ask that any concerns about the father or the child be shared as they arise so you can help address them. By establishing a neutral relationship,

Tips for Working with Service Providers

➤ Understand confidentiality rules for mental health professionals and make sure you have the appropriate information releases (this could include releases from the child welfare agency if the child is involved in the services).

➤ In the initial contact, spend more time listening than talking. This will show the service provider you respect their position and lay the foundation for a working relationship. It also allows you to gather valuable information about your client, his family, and the goals of treatment.

➤ Plan ahead to talk and don't wait until the last minute and then expect information from the provider. You both have very busy caseloads and likely have different schedules; the provider may often work evenings and weekends.

➤ Do not assume you have the same goals. Ask the provider about the treatment goals. If they conflict with or diverge from the legal case, discuss the perceived conflict and see if there is a way to address it.

➤ Know the rules of the agency and what will disqualify your client for services if you are helping him get services on his own.

➤ Remember you have a different frame of reference from service providers. You see what the court expects of your client and want to know why the agency isn't providing services to get him there. The service providers will stress "meeting the client where he is," meaning they will require him to show he wants to be in services and work toward those goals.

you lay the foundation for the caseworker to be receptive to your concerns as the case progresses. If you work together, the caseworker is more likely to return your phone calls, answer your questions, and listen to your client's concerns and progress.

One approach with caseworkers is to ask them to identify your client's strengths and areas for improvement. You can also ask what the caseworker's goal is for your client. If the worker wants your client to go to a certain service and you know a reputable provider, ask if the worker knows the provider. ("Has your agency ever worked with the North Benton Counseling Agency that Walter Evans coordinates?") While the first meeting may not be the time to demand a particular service provider, discussing the issue generally lets the worker know you are listening and you have knowledge that may be useful in crafting a solution.

Discussions with caseworkers also provide an opportunity to show your client understands his child's needs. If you and your client have talked about assessing the child's needs through special education or early intervention services, share his ideas with the caseworker or have the father do so when you meet with the caseworker. This shows that your client can focus on the child's needs. The next time the case is in court, this is a positive fact to bring up. ("After court last month Aaron asked you if Vanessa could be evaluated for an IEP.") If the father goes to an IEP meeting, bring that to the attention of the caseworker and the court.

Helping the worker understand your client

Historically, nonresident fathers have played a small role, if any, in child welfare cases.[5] Caseworkers are often not used to working with fathers. As a result, they may resist placement with the father or may not be used to listening to a father's wishes regarding placement and services.[6] If you have social workers in your office, use their expertise to communicate your client's position and needs to the caseworker. (See *Social Work—Lawyer Teams* box.) In one situation, a nonresident father wanted his mother to be the placement for his infant son who was originally placed in a nonrelative home. The agency did not want to consider moving the child. Through several conversations with the caseworker, the social worker was able to address each of the agency's concerns—attachment, stability, space in the grandmother's home, contact with other family members—from a social work perspective and was able to show the agency that placement with the grandmother was clinically the best decision for the family.

Getting to know the caseworker

It helps to understand the caseworker's expertise on issues in a case. Child welfare cases often involve such issues as substance abuse, developmental delays, and mental health treatment. Do not assume the caseworker is an expert in these issues. Caseworkers have a variety of education and experience, so learning their backgrounds can help you decide how to approach them. Is the worker skilled and knowledgeable about the issues specific to your client's child welfare case? If so, seek the caseworker's input on those issues. If not, you or someone with this knowledge may need to educate the worker. If your office has a social worker with expertise in this area, she can discuss these issues with the worker in a non-threatening way. This can be an asset especially if your client is dealing with an issue like mental illness or substance dependency, which agencies can see as barriers for your client.

Social Work—Lawyer Teams

When representing nonresident fathers, it can be advantageous to have a social worker in your office who can:

➤ provide insight into the mental health and social service needs of your client;

➤ assist in advocacy with the agency;

➤ participate in staffings; and

➤ help your client develop and clarify goals.

A social worker can assist you:

1) **when working with a difficult client or when you need to try a different approach.** For example, in one case Michael was repeatedly venting his frustrations to the caseworker and then calling his lawyer with a crisis when the agency reacted negatively toward him. Michael's lawyer consulted the social worker in his office. The social worker recommended calling Michael at the beginning of each week to discuss the case instead of waiting for Michael to call in crisis. The lawyer developed a lawyer-client relationship based on planning instead of crises. The father, feeling supported and empowered, was then able to make progress toward his goal of having the child placed in his care.

2) **when participating in case staffings.** For example, a lawyer was attending a staffing regarding a psychological assessment of her client, John. The assessment concluded John had no capacity to care for himself or others. A social worker attended the staffing with the lawyer. She explained to the clinical reviewer some problems with the original testing, such as how John's anxiety interfered with the results, the unreliability and inappropriateness with some of the tests performed, and basic questions or observations the psychologist should have made that contradicted some information in her report. She successfully advocated for a parenting capacity assessment as the more appropriate evaluation.

These two examples show how having a social work-lawyer team can benefit the representation the lawyer provides the client.

Sources:
Washington State Office of Public Defense Parents Representation Program. *Social Worker Practice Standards,* found at www.opd.wa.gov/PRP-home.htm; Anderson, Alexis, Lynn Barenberg and Paul R. Tremblay. "Professional Ethics in Interdisciplinary Collaboratives: Zeal, Paternalism and Mandated Reporting." *Clinical Law Review,* Spring 2007, Boston College Law School Research Paper No. 101, NYLS Clinical Research Institute Paper No. 06/07-4. Available at SSRN: http://ssrn.com.

Sharing positive stories

Another way to help a caseworker understand your client is sharing a positive story about your client's interactions with his child. Stories have two advantages over attempts to persuade by argument. First, they reflect an event that actually happened and are client-focused instead of lawyer-focused. They tell what your client did with his child, not his lawyer's view of him. Caseworkers expect you to argue on behalf of your client. A story is less adversarial, in part because it relates an event that occurred, rather than a legal argument. Stories also create a lasting image in the minds of caseworkers and other professionals who hear them.

To use stories, begin by making sure the client knows and consents to what you are going to share. Let him know why you are telling the story to the worker. Choose a story that exemplifies a critical issue in the case such as attachment despite separation, or the ability to focus on what is important for a child. For example, one father had been separated from his children for 10 months without visitation because of his confusion about the role he could play and administrative bungling. When he finally had a chance to visit with his children, he brought the toy trucks the boys had liked to play with before the separation. He walked in the office and the boys saw the trucks and shouted, "Daddy, daddy, you remembered our favorite trucks!" as they ran up and hugged him. The lawyer shared that story with every new caseworker or therapist after they became involved in the case as an example of the attachment the boys and their father shared. The story told the worker more about the parent-child relationship than a three-hour dissertation defense in court.

Communicating client concerns

You can help resolve barriers to your client's goals by communicating his concerns to the caseworkers. This requires more than listening to fathers and passing along complaints to caseworkers. It involves clarifying with the client what he wants, then proposing solutions to him and the caseworker.

Listening and clarifying information

Parents in child welfare cases often complain to their lawyers about their case. Listening to the client is critical in a child welfare case because you are often the only person the father can talk to without fear that venting frustrations will hurt or sabotage his case. When a client complains for 10 minutes about visitation, first listen. Then show you understand by framing what he has said: "So you are saying that you want the visit at a location you can get to on one bus instead of three." Next ask the client if he wants to find a solution to the problem, or if he was just expressing anger about the situation. This step is important to ensure the father really wants to solve the problem and will work with the caseworker. It also involves the father in devising the solution, rather than relying on you and the caseworker to solve it for him. It also helps him assume responsibility in a positive, nonthreatening way.

Working with a father to develop solutions also avoids problems. If he was just expressing frustration with visitation, he may have left out important details, such as his not calling the caseworker ahead of time to confirm a visit. If you simply relay the father's frustration to the worker without checking the details, you may later learn from the caseworker that the client has not taken the steps he agreed to—missing an appointment or failing to schedule a visit. When you sound surprised, the worker may believe the father misled you. When you then call the father to express your frustration with the confusion, he may become defensive or believe that rather than helping him, you are yet another "member of the system" siding with the caseworker. Clarifying what the father wants and developing a plan together forces you to discuss the issues in more detail, and avoid these dangers.

When you call the caseworker, focus your conversation on the solution rather than the complaint. This helps the caseworker feel like part of the solution. Suggest solutions your client agrees with, but be prepared to listen to the caseworker's response and ideas first. You do not need to agree with the caseworker, but listening and acknowledging you understand goes a long way. In addition to the caseworker being more willing to listen to your proposed solutions, it lets you gather information about the case and the agency's view of your client.

While solution-based problem solving is a good start, it will not always lead to success. Some caseworkers will be defensive no matter what you say. Sometimes the agency's view of your client will be shaped by prejudices about fathers, or the client's past mistakes. Other times, the caseworker will ignore your attempts to communicate or will refuse to work with you. In these situations, you may need to speak to the caseworker's supervisor. When going up the administrative ladder, it is important to know both who is in the chain of command and the written rules or procedures that govern the agency. Some child welfare agencies (especially those administered statewide) will have written rules that govern the services agencies are required to provide. Other states list them in statutes. Finally, some state court systems allow you to bring complaints to the court either through motions on issues like visitation or specific services, or through motions asking the court to find the agency has failed to make reasonable efforts.

When all attempts to work with the agency have failed and the problem is negatively affecting your client's ability to work toward his goals, you may need to consider administrative approaches or request court intervention. You should also use a solution-based approach in drafting and presenting a motion. Rather than just asking a judge to make a negative finding to slap an agency's wrists, your motion should propose a way to fix the problem. When you ask for a finding of no reasonable efforts because an agency failed to provide adequate visitation services, you should also show what your client wants—visitation scheduled around his work hours.

Setting boundaries

One final thing to keep in mind as you are working with your client's caseworker is setting appropriate boundaries. It will help you gather information about the case and the agency's view of your client if you are friendly with the caseworker. But you must be careful not to compromise your relationship with your client. Do this by being a good listener without sharing your client's confidences. Similarly, you may need to tell the caseworker about how your client's mental health impacts his daily living without revealing detailed personal information that the agency doesn't already know. This can often be accomplished by discussing general expectations for a person in recovery from alcoholism, for example, and what supports have helped others in similar situations.

Child Welfare Staffings

The term "child welfare staffing" refers to the numerous meetings between caseworkers, clients, service providers, and sometimes lawyers that occur throughout the child welfare case. Some occur informally among child welfare agency staff alone, such as when a worker meets with her supervisor to discuss case issues. Some are required by state law or rules, such as meetings to decide major issues in a case such as return home.[7] Agencies use staffings to develop case plans with parents and to develop special education plans for children. Remind your client throughout the case to tell you about any upcoming meetings he has with agency staff and be sure to regularly ask his caseworkers about upcoming meetings. You can also suggest a meeting to discuss issues. When you learn about a meeting, ask if you can attend. If the child welfare agency has rules outlining meetings, such as child and family team meetings or case reviews, find out whether lawyers can attend. Many of the skills lawyers need at these staffings are similar, regardless of the type of staffing.

Preparing for staffings

While staffings can appear to be "one more thing" for you to do, they provide opportunities to advocate for your client and move the case toward his goals.

Once you learn about a staffing, prepare for it by learning its purpose, who requested it, and who will be present. Obtain this information from the agency caseworker or the child's lawyer. Before any staffing, review your client's goals with him and discuss what information you may or may not share.

Plan what information you will communicate at the staffing, how you respond to information presented, and when you will argue and when you will listen. It is empowering for your client to understand this ahead of time. It helps him know that if you choose not to bring up a concern it does not mean you will never bring it up. Instead, it simply means that one set point in the meeting is not the most advantageous time to do so. Make a list of the client's key concerns, as well as ones you think are important. Then discuss the list with the client and prioritize them. Alert the client that you may bring up issues or stories that you think will help his case. ("I know you have heard the toy truck story many times, but it is important for this group to hear it so they understand how focused you are on your children.") Finally, develop a way for your client to let you know if he wants to talk to you alone during the meeting. The social service staff at the meeting might interpret a client's request to talk to his lawyer negatively ("What is he hiding?"). Because of this, if your client gives you a signal indicating he wants to talk, tell the staff that *you* want to talk to your client. ("I need to talk with Aaron about something; could you give us a minute?") Better that they draw mistaken inferences about you than your client.

Additionally, if the staffing allows the father to bring other supportive relatives, encourage him to do so. In one case, a father received emotional support and consistent feedback from his girlfriend, a leader of a neighborhood community organization. She came to every staffing with him, never saying more than one or two things. Her presence, however, helped the father in two ways. First, her being at the meeting made him more at ease, which in turn helped him to speak more clearly and calmly about his concerns. Second, it told the caseworkers that he was able to have a healthy relationship with a woman who was a positive force in the community.

Defining your roles

When the staffing begins, make a simple diagram of the names and titles of everyone at the table. That way you will know who the players are and their roles without repeatedly asking. Have a notepad, but don't take detailed notes—record only what is important.

Advocating for the father's position requires you to move beyond being a mouthpiece for your client. While you remain an advocate at the staffing, the roles you play differ from those in court. No rules of evidence or procedure govern the staffing, so you can ask leading or open-ended questions. Remember that your role can be flexible, and that you can wear different hats during a meeting. These include being a sounding board for your client's concerns, developing plans the client can follow, and serving as a translator by explaining the child welfare system's rules and requirements to the father and explaining the father and his relationship to his child to those in the system.

Translator

As a translator, you will often have to explain some of the staff's language to the client so he can understand. At one staffing, the social work staff kept wondering if the client had "anecdotals" about his son. Neither the father nor his lawyer understood what the agency wanted, so the lawyer asked. Doing so made the lawyer look confused, not the client. The agency was looking for stories that exemplified the child's problems with attention deficit disorder. The client was then able to rattle off story after story of the child's previous problems with staying on task, and how the client sought help for the child. Similar instances occur when agency staff use agency jargon. A caseworker asks, "Do you understand all the issues in your 600?" The father needs to know that the "600" is the case plan the workers are asking him to follow.

Advocate

In your advocacy role, sometimes you will find yourself playing the bad lawyer with good intentions. The goal of this role is to take the agency's heat for demanding things, instead of the client. If you know the agency should be following a visitation rule that requires it to arrange visitation weekly, say so. If the agency makes excuses, empathize while stressing it must follow the rules. As your client's lawyer, you need to take the legal steps available, administratively or in court, to compel them to follow the rules. Once again, it is better that the agency get angry with you for pushing the rules, than at your client.

Facilitator

You may also be a facilitator. Look for opportunities for your client to explain his concerns to the agency staff. You can respond to a worker's concerns by asking your client to talk about a particular issue. For example, when a worker says she wants your client to attend family therapy at a specific time, and you know the client's work schedule is inflexible that night, you can ask the client to explain. "Andre, could you tell Ms. Munson why you have to stay late on Wednesdays?"

Similarly, if a staffing is focusing on why a father wants his brother to be the children's placement, asking the father to tell the worker about how the brother and his wife successfully raised their own children can accomplish several goals. It empowers the father, who is able to speak positively about his family, and tells the social service staff that the client can describe what positive parenting looks like. It also describes the family's ability to care for children. Finally, it creates another opportunity for you to bring your client's out-of-court work into the courtroom when you question the worker. ("Do you remember Aaron being at the April 6 staffing? On that date, he said he could not do therapy on Wednesday afternoons because he had to work late.")

Storyteller

Sometimes it helps to return to your role as a storyteller at the staffing, using vignettes about the client and child to make points, show a skill the client has learned, or highlight his ability to advocate for his child's needs. In addition to you directly telling a story, you can also ask the caseworkers who have responded to your client positively to tell the group what they have seen on visits or at other parent-child interactions. For example, a therapist had heard the foster parents tell a story about how a three-year-old child showed attachment by letting her father (and not anyone else) sit with her on her favorite blanket. When the therapist told the story to those at the staffing it showed far more about their relationship than merely saying the father and daughter had a positive attachment.

Negotiator

The lack of formal rules at a staffing lets you, at times, get to a point you want to reach and negotiate a desired outcome. In Aaron's example, discussed earlier, the agency wanted a meeting to convince him to sign consents to adoption. Aaron brought his father (a retired police officer) and his lawyer to the staffing. When the agency started with its goal, the lawyer, Aaron, and his father were able to bring the conversation around to the grandfather's availability as a placement option and a state requirement that the agency consider relatives. When a worker later discovered concerns about the nonrelative foster parents, Aaron's father became the logical and safe place for the children to live.

Closing the staffing

At the end of the staffing, if an agreement has been reached, confirm it verbally at the meeting then promptly follow up with a letter. Confirm other important issues such as work/therapy conflicts. The letter should not be confrontational. ("Thank you for agreeing to increase Mr. Wilson's visits to twice a week and understanding that his work conflicts with scheduling therapy on a Wednesday.")

Such language confirms the end result better than legalese and supports a positive long-term relationship between your client and the agency.

If a meeting is designed to create or amend a case plan or other written document, be sure your client and you agree that the case plan tasks further your client's goals and the well-being of the child. Also be sure that the client can meet the tasks. If you disagree with a proposal, frame your disagreements in terms of the child's interests as well. ("From a three year old's perspective, the visit should be in a place where he can have fun and play with his dad, not at a table in a busy McDonald's.") Before signing the plan, ask to talk with your client to review the proposed plan. Ask him if he is sure he can take the steps the agency is asking him to take. Tell him this is the time to ask for other changes if he wants them.

Bringing Information to the Court

Each time you go to court, have a list of things you want the court to hear about your client. These might include his attendance at school events, his new insight into an issue in therapy, his plan to present his father as a placement option, or his clean drug screens. Because child welfare cases can occur over a long period, it is important to let the judge know the positives about your client every chance you get.

Look for opportunities to bring information about the father to the court's attention. Give details at the hearing, such as at a permanency hearing where a client's positive visitation and follow-through with services are relevant. If it is not directly relevant, such as at a status hearing on procedural issues, mention it quickly and ask the court if it wants testimony. For example, if a case is just up for discovery status you can say, "Judge, I just wanted to let you know that Mr. Wilson was at his son's IEP meeting last week. Because he was not the foster parent, he did not have final say on the plan, but could provide input. If you want testimony on the issue he can provide it. . . ." As noted earlier, you can use the information gathered at staffings, such as discussions or agreements about visitation or services, in court. Since your client was present, he can confirm conversations even if agency staff balk at it. You can also use your confirming letter or written agreements.

Court dates are also important for fathers who are not making progress. They become the first step in revisiting the issue of responsibility. When a judge hears a father has not followed through on visitation or treatment, schedule a meeting with the client to figure out his future relationship with his child and the future of the case. This needs to be more than words in passing in the hall as you leave the court. Remind him directly that when you began working together, you told him that it was his responsibility to take steps to visit the child. Tell him again that when a judge hears he is not visiting, it tells the judge he doesn't want to be involved in the child's life. When he protests, tell him that your job as a lawyer is to tell him what he needs to do to persuade the judge—and not showing up at visits or therapy sends the wrong message. Remind him that part of your job is to bring all the positive steps he has taken to the judge's attention, and that when he has not taken those steps, you have nothing good to tell the judge.

> "I've never felt how I felt when …my son was born…he's changed my life…. I got this second shift job when he was born, and I've had it for almost three years now. It's changed my life a lot…. He's really shown me what love is."
>
> —*Nonresident father*

Next, give him a reality check. Ask him what he wants. Does he really want custody? Let him know that he is free to take another path. If he wants custody, he needs to change. Whatever his goal, explore the concrete steps needed to achieve that goal, and have him decide if he is committed to taking those steps. If he says he wants custody, or increased visitation, ask him what he thinks he has to do to achieve that goal. If he wants his mother to become the child's substitute care provider, discuss steps to achieve that goal. Ask him if he is going to take those steps. If he says he will attend visitation, go to a doctor's visit with the child, or call his mother, tell him to call you immediately after the event. When he calls after following through, give positive feedback. ("Now that's something we can let the judge know.")

Conclusion

As a lawyer for a nonresident father you can help your client and his children in a number of ways. If your work helps him achieve custody of his child, you may believe that you have accomplished a victory. But custody is just one possible positive outcome. A father may be happy to see his child raised by a grandparent or supportive foster parent. A father of an adolescent in residential care may decide it is better to support his child through visitation, and as a placement resource for the future. What remains consistent throughout your work, however, is your role: helping your client explore and choose from his legal options, working together to identify the steps he needs to achieve those goals, and bringing his progress to the attention of the court and other decision makers.

The author thanks Debbie and Marty and the staff and clients of the Children's Law Project of the Legal Assistance Foundation of Chicago for their help in developing this chapter.

Endnotes

1. For a discussion of genograms in child welfare cases, *see* Koh Peters, Jean. *Representing Children in Child Protective Proceedings: Ethical and Practical Dimensions,* 3d ed. Lexis Law Publishing, 2007, 114-119.

2. Recent research shows that children in kinship care have significantly fewer placement shifts than children in nonrelative foster care, are less likely to remain in foster care or to have additional allegations of abuse or neglect, and are more likely to achieve reunification. Winokur, M. et al. "Matched Comparison of Children in Kinship Care and Foster Care on Child Welfare Outcomes." *Families in Society: The Journal of Contemporary Social Sciences* 89, 2008, 338-346.

3. Section 103 of the Fostering Connections to Success Act, P.L. 110-151 (2008), now requires that "within 30 days after the removal of a child from the custody of the parent or parents of the child, the State shall exercise due diligence to identify and provide notice to all adult grandparents and other adult relatives of the child . . . subject to exceptions due to family or domestic violence." Notice must be provided of the child welfare case and how relatives can become involved in the care of the child.

4. "Arguably . . . the most significant and central question in most dependency cases is not whether a parent committed "neglect" but whether and when a child can return home safely." Cohen, J. and M. Cortese. "Cornerstone Advocacy in the First 60 Days: Achieving Safe and Lasting Reunification for Families." *ABA Child Law Practice* 28(3), May 2009, 34.

5. Malm, K., J. Murray and R. Geen. *What about the Dads? Child Welfare Agencies' Efforts to Identify, Locate and Involve Nonresident Fathers.* Washington, D.C.: U.S. Department of Health and Human Services, Office of the Assistant Secretary of Planning and Evaluation, 2006.

6. Ibid.

7. In some circumstances, these staffings include mediation, case reviews, clinical reviews, case plan reviews, and staff decision-making meetings. They can even be child and family team meetings, and family decision-making meetings. States and agencies have different names for staffings and use them for various purposes.

CHAPTER FOUR

Representing Nonresident Fathers in Dependency Cases

Andrew L. Cohen

CHECKLIST

Representing Nonresident Fathers in Dependency Cases

Fight for custody if your client wishes.

➤ Inform the agency of the father's interest in custody promptly.

➤ Remind the agency of the father's interest in custody throughout the case.

➤ Request a concurrent goal of custody with the father.

Ensure successful visits.

➤ If necessary, seek court-ordered visitation based on the agency's "reasonable efforts" obligations.

➤ Encourage the father to:

  ➤ accept every visit offered;

  ➤ avoid arriving late or leaving early;

  ➤ confirm visits in advance;

  ➤ call the caseworker if an emergency prevents him from attending; and

  ➤ alert you if transportation to visits is an issue.

➤ Press the agency for a more accessible visit location or schedule if necessary.

➤ Request longer, more frequent visits as the case progresses.

➤ Work with the caseworker, father and (when appropriate) a counselor if visits go poorly.

Prove the father's fitness to parent at trial.

➤ Offer evidence of your client's *physical capacity* to parent by showing he:

  ➤ has safe and appropriate housing;

  ➤ has sufficient financial resources;

➤ has access to child care or school for the child, if necessary; and

➤ will be able to access services he and the child need once the case closes.

➤ Show your client understands and can meet the child's physical and emotional needs (e.g., his *parenting capacity*). Evidence could include:

➤ competent full- or part-time caretaking of other children;

➤ progress on a case plan;

➤ a responsive attitude to the child at visitation and/or before the case.

Help fathers who do not want custody achieve their other goals.

➤ If the father wants his child placed with a relative:

➤ Ensure the agency knows the client's wishes.

➤ Urge the placement resource to contact the social worker.

➤ File appropriate petitions on behalf of the resource (if appropriate).

➤ If the father supports the mother's efforts to regain custody:

➤ Work closely with mother's counsel.

➤ Urge the father to maintain a positive relationship with the mother.

➤ If the father wants contact with his child once the case ends:

➤ Try to obtain a written agreement or court order for visitation or other contact.

➤ If your jurisdiction allows, advocate for an open adoption or postadoption visitation order.

➤ Explain the fragility of informal arrangements and postadoption orders.

Download this and other checklists at **www.fatherhoodqic.org/checklists**

You've just met your client, a nonresident father who has little or no relationship with the child who is the subject of the child welfare case. He has not paid child support and has never visited the child. Will the judge and the child welfare agency caseworkers believe your client can play a meaningful role in the child's life? Will they ever trust that he can succeed as a custodial parent? Unless the father receives services to learn to parent, he is likely to fail, especially given the complexities of parenting children with histories of abuse or neglect. As his lawyer, your advocacy is critical to help the court and agency see the father as a viable permanency resource for the child.

This chapter offers practical guidance to counsel for the nonresident father seeking custody of the child or some other custodial arrangement that would let him maintain an ongoing relationship with his child (e.g., kinship care with a paternal relative or open adoption). It assumes the nonresident father is not the "offending" parent in the dependency case, and that he has appeared in court and is working cooperatively with appointed counsel. (See *Locating Your Client* box.)

Protecting Your Client's Standing

At the earliest opportunity, you must determine the father's legal status regarding the child. In some jurisdictions, only "legal" fathers receive notice of dependency proceedings and are appointed counsel. In others, courts also appoint counsel for putative fathers identified by the agency on its dependency petition or by the mother. That appointment—and the client's standing to participate in the case—may be short-lived. Putative fathers may have only a small window of time in which to establish paternity; their right to participate in the dependency proceeding may also be severely curtailed until they establish paternity.[1] (See Chapter 1, *Advocating for the Constitutional Rights of Nonresident Fathers.*)

Determine whether the client is, or ever was, married to the child's mother. Try to obtain a copy of the child's birth certificate.[2] In some jurisdictions, the father's name on the birth certificate may be sufficient to assure the client full parental rights or standing to participate in the proceeding. But if the client's name is not on the birth certificate, or his presence alone is insufficient to protect the client's standing, you may need to help your client establish paternity in the dependency court (if it has jurisdiction) or in another court.

The agency may also challenge the father's standing, or right to contest the proceedings, based on abandonment, nonsupport of the child, or failure to establish a meaningful relationship with the child.[3] Become familiar with the statutory and common law definitions of these terms. When the client's standing and right to participate are at issue, you'll need to work quickly with your client to show the court a history of contact with the child (or an explanation for lack of contact) and/or evidence of payment of formal child support or informal assistance.

Advocating for Your Client's Goals

Communicate regularly with your client. Fully explain the nature of the dependency process and the risks and benefits of cooperating or fighting with the agency. Only after such full disclosure can the client make an informed decision about his goals.

Explain the potential "incidental" outcomes of the case. For example, the dependency court may have jurisdiction to order the client to pay child support to the child's custodian or the costs of foster care to the state. If the client is in the country illegally, he may be subject to seizure and eventual deportation if he appears at court. Similarly, he may be held on any outstanding criminal warrants if he appears. Such information may play an important part in the client's decision making.

The fully-informed nonresident father may want to:

- seek custody of his child;
- have a relative or other person care for or adopt the child;
- have the mother regain custody; or
- have visits with his child regardless of the dispositional outcome of the case.

Fighting for custody

The first step when the nonresident father is seeking custody is to inform the agency of the client's goal. The caseworker may not be familiar with the father or be aware of his interest. If the conduct of the mother leading to agency intervention was egregious, or if she refuses to cooperate with services, the agency may focus on placing the child with the father. (For guidance when the father lives out of state, see *The Interstate Compact on the Placement of Children* box.) Even if the agency is seeking to return the child to the mother or is seeking an alternative plan, constantly remind the agency of the father's interest and request that it consider a concurrent goal of custody by the father. The agency's goals often change and courts often rule against parents who are perceived to have abandoned their efforts to work cooperatively with the agency.

Locating Your Client: A Checklist

Even when a nonresident father does not formally appear in a case, courts in many jurisdictions will appoint counsel if the father is identified by the mother or by the agency in its complaint or petition. If you are appointed to represent a nonresident father, your first task may be to locate him.

Because you cannot take a position in court on behalf of a parent you have not met, make every effort to contact the father and learn his position quickly. The clock begins ticking toward permanency under the Adoption and Safe Families Act (ASFA) as soon as the child enters state care;[1] it does not wait until the father is located, served with notice, or appears.

The father's address may be on the agency's petition. If not, the mother, the agency caseworker, or even the child may know his whereabouts. If these inquiries are unsuccessful, consider the following options:

➤ Send a letter to the last known address informing the client of the proceeding and instructing him to contact counsel immediately.

➤ Send letters to any of the client's relatives (if such relatives are identified in the agency file, or if the social worker, the mother, or even the child knows where they reside), asking them to have the father contact counsel immediately regarding the case.

➤ Leave a sealed letter at the father's last known address with a separate cover note requesting that the landlord or current resident forward the letter to the father.

➤ Consult the phone book covering the area of the last known address.

➤ Consult Web sites that focus on addresses and phone numbers, such as whitepages.com, mamma.com, or addresses.com.

➤ Consult the state Department of Revenue or other child support agency to determine if it has an address for the father on file.

➤ Contact the state Department of Corrections, or access inmate-locator Web sites, such as VINElink (www.vinelink.com), the Corrections Connection (www.corrections.com/links/show/20), the Pampered Prisoner (www.thepamperedprisoner.com/inmatesearch.htm), or the Federal Bureau of Prisons inmate locator service (www.bop.gov/iloc2/LocateInmate.jsp), to determine if the father is currently residing in a correctional facility.

➤ Retain the services of a private investigator to locate him, at court expense, if your state allows.

If all reasonable efforts to locate the client are unsuccessful, insist on service of process by publication or other notice that complies with state law. Wait for any "objection" or "appearance" deadline to expire. If the father still does not appear or contact you, the court is likely to strike your appearance. If it does not, you may wish to withdraw from the representation, or take no position in the proceeding but protect the client's rights to the extent possible.

Source:

1. The court must hold a "permanency hearing" within 12 months of a child entering foster care to decide the permanent plan for the child. *See* P.L. 105-89, § 302, amending 42 U.S.C. § 675(5)C).

Visitation

Whether or not the agency supports the father's goal of obtaining custody, the father must make every effort to maintain a relationship with the child through regular and frequent visitation. If the father had little contact with the child before court involvement, he may have to *create* a parenting relationship through visitation.

Getting visits. The agency's obligation to provide "reasonable efforts" toward family reunification means, first and foremost, that it provide parent-child visitation. As a corollary to the agency's obligation to provide visits, the parent must attend them; that is, most courts view regular attendance at visitation as one of the most important signs of the parent's commitment to the child. To the extent possible, the father should accept every visit offered to him. He should also attend each visit for its duration and not show up late or leave early. Explain to him that, if he is going to be late to a visit or miss it, he must call the agency caseworker or foster parent immediately.

If the agency refuses to give the father visits, immediately seek court assistance. Speed is of the essence. Attachments can be lost if months go by with little or no visitation. During those months, the child forms attachments with other caretakers. The earlier and more assertively the client seeks visitation, the more likely the agency and the court are to act on his requests.

Getting to visits. When the agency has custody of the child, parent-child visits are usually—at least at the beginning of the case—at the agency office or a supervised visitation center. Make sure your client can get to the visits. If the father does not drive or have a car, he must get a reliable ride or use public transportation. If transportation is unavailable to the agency office or visitation center, press the social worker to hold visits in a more accessible location. If the

The Interstate Compact on the Placement of Children

Nonresident fathers living out of state face another barrier to reunification or placement with their children. Many jurisdictions interpret the Interstate Compact on the Placement of Children (ICPC) to apply to out-of-state nonresident parents.

The ICPC requires that the *receiving state* (state where the nonresident parent lives) conduct a home study of the out-of-state placement before the *sending state* (state hearing the dependency case) can place the child across state lines. Such home studies may take weeks, or even months, to complete. As a result, if a child is removed from a mother in New York City, a father in Hoboken, NJ may have to wait months to get his child, even though the parents live just a few miles apart and neither state alleges the father is unfit.

For a thorough discussion of the ICPC's impact on out-of-state parents, see:

➤ Sankaran, Vivek S. "Navigating the Interstate Compact on the Placement of Children: Advocacy Tips for Child Welfare Attorneys." *ABA Child Law Practice* 27(3), May 2008, 33.

➤ Sankaran, Vivek S. "Out of State and Out of Luck: The Treatment of Non-Custodial Parents under the Interstate Compact on the Placement of Children." *Yale Law & Policy Review* 25, Fall 2006, 63.

➤ Fiermonte, Cecilia. "Interstate Placements: Applying the ICPC." *ABA Child Law Practice* 21(5), July 2002, 65.

worker balks at this, seek court assistance by filing a motion for visitation or other motion arguing that the agency is not providing reasonable efforts to re-unify the family.

The agency often schedules visits only during weekday business hours. This arrangement may conflict with your client's work schedule. Explain to your client that attending visits is crucial. If your client cannot take time off from work, urge the social worker to hold visits after hours or on weekends. If the agency cannot accommodate your request, recommend having another agency or supervised visitation center with extended hours supervise the visits. Alternatively, propose having a friend or relative of the father supervise the visits. Again, if the worker is not willing to accommodate this request, seek redress in court.

Confirming visits. The agency often requires parents to call to confirm shortly before the visit or the visit will be canceled. Urge your client to faithfully confirm. The agency usually has no obligation to "make up" a visit cancelled for failure to confirm. Last-minute cancellations disappoint children and suggest to the agency and the court that the parent lacks commitment and is unreliable.

Of course, parents often miss visits for valid reasons, such as illness or family emergencies. Advise your client to contact the worker as soon as possible of the need to cancel. If a cancellation occurs, be sure to document the reason in case the matter arises later in court or in an agency internal review.

Getting more visits. The agency may offer the father weekly visitation. Some agencies offer visitation only every other week or, worse, monthly. Visitation for incarcerated parents may be even less frequent. (Chapter 8 discusses visitation for incarcerated fathers.) Needless to say, it is difficult to preserve attachments, and almost impossible to create them, on such a schedule. And frequent and regular visitation is particularly important for very young children.[4]

Advocate strenuously for more frequent parent-child visitation for the father seeking custody. Address this first with the social worker,[5] who may agree to a plan with progressively more frequent visits depending on the father's cooperation with services and attendance at visits. If the worker is not willing to provide more frequent visitation, consider appeals to supervisors and more senior agency staff. Be sure to document these efforts in a letter to the agency from you or your client.

If efforts with the agency prove unavailing, seek help from the court. This requires familiarity with relevant legal standards for visitation requests. In some jurisdictions, judges can order the agency to provide whatever visitation they believe serves the child's best interests.[6] In others, courts may not be able to do so unless the moving party proves the agency has abused its discretion or erred as a matter of law.[7] Whatever the standard, judges may hesitate to "overrule" the agency's visitation decisions. Consider retaining an expert to help you prove the benefits of more frequent visitation. Offer your court affidavits, research, or articles on the benefits of visitation to the extent permitted by your local practice and rules of evidence.[8]

Visits with the unwilling child. If the child does not want visits, or reacts poorly to them, your client may be perceived as selfish and uncaring if he pushes too hard for visitation. Even when the child wants to visit, the child may treat her father coldly, or shrink from him during visits, which may be very disappointing for your client. Still, the father must not give up; there may be many reasons for the child's feelings or reactions. Work to identify those reasons by asking the worker to explain to the father why the child may be reacting this way. In certain circumstances, it may help to seek permission to speak to or meet with the child's therapist and foster parents, to discuss these matters further. Sometimes "therapeutic" visits—visits with the child's therapist or other counselor present to help the father respond to the child's needs—may be appropriate.

Press the agency to determine how the father can be introduced or reintroduced into the child's life positively. If the agency does not cooperate, notify the court, arguing that "reasonable efforts" requires the agency to determine how the father can visit the child to further family reunification efforts and serve the child's interests.

Services

Compliance with the agency's case plan is usually the best way to convince the agency to place the child with the nonresident father. Even if the agency has other plans, courts may still order such placement if the father has complied with a case plan. It is crucial, therefore, that the agency provide the father a case plan with appropriate services.

Getting a case plan. Getting a case plan from the agency is easy if the agency is interested in placement with the father. If the agency has other goals, you may have to advocate for the worker to create a plan for the father. If the agency is still unwilling, ask the court to order the agency to create a plan.[9] In the meantime, you may need to identify appropriate local services and help the client obtain them.

Getting the right services. Getting a case plan is not enough. The father must get the *right* services, participate in those services, and learn from them how to parent the child. The agency is often willing to negotiate case plans with parents. You can help the father negotiate the plan with his worker to secure the services he feels are most helpful to him. In addition to regular and frequent visitation, most fathers benefit from some form of parenting education. Even if the father has parenting experience, completing a parenting program will help him convince the agency and the court that he has the desire and skills to parent the child. If the child has special needs, the case plan should include services that teach the father how to parent a child with those needs.

Many fathers need assistance with job skills and finding employment. It is difficult for any parent to care for a child without regular income. Press the agency caseworker to make all necessary referrals to agencies specializing in job training and placement.

If the plan requires the father to do too much, he is likely to fail. If it contains too few tasks—or the *wrong* tasks—he will not be able to parent the child even if he fully complies with services, and neither the agency nor the court will entrust him with the child. (See *Services Checklist* box.) Fathers may be more likely to succeed in classes and other services that are father-specific and account for men's learning and interaction styles.[10] (See Chapter 2 for more on male help-seeking behavior.)

■ Services Checklist

Counsel can serve nonresident fathers by becoming familiar with available services and providers, especially those within a short distance of the client's home or accessible by public transportation. Such services include:

➤ job training;

➤ housing assistance;

➤ parenting classes (both basic skills and skills specific to the needs of the child); and

➤ help procuring state and/or federal benefits for the father and/or the child, including food stamps.

Other fathers may need:

➤ substance abuse counseling, including Alcoholics Anonymous or Narcotics Anonymous;

➤ mental health services, including counseling and psychiatric assistance;

➤ anger-management counseling;

➤ batterer's treatment;

➤ sex offender treatment; and

➤ referrals to low-cost or pro bono legal services for matters other than the dependency proceeding, such as housing or immigration.

Child Support

Many nonresident fathers are subject to child support orders. Some have been paying; others have not. Many dependency courts have jurisdiction to enter and/or modify support orders. Inform your client that by appearing in the case he may be subject to such orders.

Paying child support allows fathers to show their commitment to the child. In many jurisdictions, failure to pay support is grounds to terminate parental rights. Paying off arrearages and making ongoing payments may be key to the father's bid for custody. (See Chapter 7 for more on child support issues.)

Trial Tips

To permanently deprive a nonresident father of custody and/or terminate his parental rights, the agency must prove he is unfit.[11] Even if the agency has no evidence of unfitness or the evidence against the father is slim, the agency may still oppose the father's request for custody. While the burden of proof is on the state,

How Child Advocates Can Better Engage Fathers in Child Welfare Cases

➤ Encourage the court and child welfare agency to make ongoing, diligent attempts to locate a missing or unknown nonresident father.

➤ Request information from the father's counsel about his intentions regarding custody of the child or maintaining or establishing a relationship with the child.

➤ Ask the father's counsel about paternal relatives who may want to maintain a relationship with the child.

➤ Ensure the child welfare agency is offering the father and his relatives meaningful services and resources to engage properly with the child.

➤ Request information from the child welfare agency about how visits between the child and father have gone.

➤ If appropriate, request information from the child about the father's or his relative's whereabouts and the child's desire to establish or maintain a relationship with them.

certain dependency courts may hesitate to entrust a child to a parent who was not previously the child's caretaker—or, perhaps, *any* child's caretaker. Some judges may even hold stereotypical views of gender roles and hesitate to place a child with *any* father. You must therefore prepare for trial with an eye to "proving fitness."

It helps to conceive of this proof as having two components:

Physical capacity looks to the mechanics of child care and is established by showing the client has:

- safe and appropriate housing for the child (such as an open room or an open bed, no lead paint if the child is young, working smoke detectors, and no "dangerous" persons in the home);
- sufficient financial resources to provide for the child (including savings, income and/or benefits);
- child care if the client works; and
- ready access (or transportation) to day care or school and to services the parent and the child need going forward.

The best proof of the father's appropriate housing is often photographs of the home, the child's bedroom and, if the child is younger, the yard and neighborhood play spaces. The father's pay stubs and/or proof of benefits are helpful to show his financial ability to care for the child.[12] In preparing the father to testify, ensure he knows the names and locations of the child's day care, school, and service providers, and how he will ensure the child's access to them should the child be placed with him.

Parenting capacity looks to the client's understanding of, and ability to meet, the child's physical and emotional needs. The father's competent full- or part-time caretaking of other children may be the most compelling evidence. Other evidence of the father's parenting capacity can include showing that he:

- understands the child's needs;
- has been kind, nurturing, and responsive to the child at visitation and/or before the case;
- successfully participated in the agency's case plan, including parenting services;
- is committed to the child (e.g., regularly attends visits, has provided ongoing child support); and
- has a "plan" for meeting the child's short- and long-term needs.

Using the client's providers as witnesses can help show that he has participated in and benefited from their programs or services. Obtaining expert assistance may also help prove the father has the skills and understanding to care for the child.

Third-party custody

The father may not want to care for the child or may acknowledge he is unable to do so. Instead, he may want a relative (e.g., his parents) or a family friend to be a foster placement for, take custody of, or adopt the child.

Explore this option with your client early in the case. Children, especially younger ones, may attach quickly to foster parents. Agencies and courts may be reluctant to sever these attachments to place children with relatives, especially absent a strong, preexisting relationship. Make sure the agency is aware of the client's wish for a kinship placement as soon as possible, and urge the placement resource to contact the social worker and fill out all necessary paperwork.

State laws and procedures may permit bypassing the foster care system by proffering the relative as a custodian, guardian, or adoptive resource for the child. As the father's counsel, you may be permitted to file the guardianship or adoption petition or other legal paperwork on behalf of the resource, or you may be restricted to a more supporting role. In either case, counsel must show—or help the petitioning resource show—that the resource has the space and finances to care for the child and the capacity to meet the child's needs.[13]

Support of the mother

If the father supports the mother's efforts to regain custody, work closely with the mother's counsel to devise a coherent, consistent strategy that presents the strongest case for the mother. You may wish to share witness examination, document review, and other trial preparation.

The mother's success at trial may depend on the father's promise of ongoing financial and child care support. Her success after trial may depend on his follow-through on those promises. Urge the father to maintain a positive relationship with the mother should she regain custody. Nonresident fathers who enjoy a good relationship with the mother tend to have greater contact and involvement with their children.[14]

Visitation rights after disposition

If the father is not seeking custody, he may wish to preserve visitation rights to the child following any dispositional order. If the child is returned to the mother, or if the custodian, guardian, or adoptive resource is the father's kin, the father may wish to address this issue informally. Discuss the possible fragility of such arrangements and the benefits of having a formal agreement or a court order for visitation.

The father may agree that the child should be adopted but want some contact with the child thereafter. Some jurisdictions allow courts to approve "open adoption" agreements or order postadoption contact.[15] Such contact may include frequent visits or visits only once or twice each year; or it may be limited to exchanging cards and photographs. Determine whether an open adoption agreement is expressly authorized or otherwise enforceable in your jurisdiction. Also warn the father about potential problems enforcing the agreement if the adoptive resource moves out of the jurisdiction or refuses to comply with the terms of the agreement.[16]

Conclusion

Representing a nonresident father is more complex than representing a custodial parent. All parents' counsel must advocate zealously for their clients' wishes. But counsel for the nonresident father is often tasked with preserving the father's standing to participate in the proceeding, convincing the agency and the court to

Surrender/Relinquishment

If you represent a father who does not want any involvement with the child, explore the reasons why. If he believes he cannot afford to raise his child, discuss the availability of job training services, child support, and assistance from the agency or other state agencies. If he believes he would be a bad parent, explain that services are available to teach him how to care for his child. If the father still does not want anything to do with the child, discuss whether he is better served by:

➤ signing a "surrender" or some other form of voluntary relinquishment, or

➤ allowing the dependency case to proceed to an uncontested termination of parental rights.

In most circumstances, the first approach is best, even though the client will have to sign paperwork, perhaps before witnesses, and may have to go to court to be questioned by the judge. Signing a voluntary relinquishment is always faster and more certain than an uncontested termination case. A dependency case may last for months or even years, and may not end in the termination of any parent's rights if the child is returned to the original caretaker or placed with a relative. Further, a parent whose rights are terminated involuntarily to one child may lose the right to reunification services regarding other—and future—children.[1]

Clients who wish to relinquish parental rights because they believe their child would be better off being adopted may be best served by actively participating in the case. The client may have strong views as to *who* should care for or adopt the child.

Fathers who sign surrender agreements or simply "disappear" from proceedings usually have no say in the placement or adoption of their children. Tell the father that, even if he has no desire to seek custody, he can participate in the proceeding to request a particular placement or adoptive resource. You may also be able to advocate for visitation or postadoption contact between the father and child if that is consistent with your client's wishes.

Fathers who wish to relinquish their rights to avoid child support present different challenges. States differ in their treatment of child support for parents who surrender their children voluntarily and those whose rights are involuntarily terminated.[2] Adoption usually ends ongoing support obligations, but it may not erase past obligations or the accrual of interest or penalties on arrearages. Know the governing law so you can explain all options to your client.[3]

Sources:

1. *See* P.L. 105-89, § 101(a)(15)(D), amending 42 U.S.C. § 671(a)(15)(D).

2. *See, e.g.*, Adoption of Marlene, 822 N.E.2d 714 (Mass. 2005) (voluntary surrender does not terminate child support obligations); County of Ventura v. Gonzales, 106 Cal. Rptr. 2d 461 (Ct. App. 2001) (order terminating parental rights also extinguishes child support obligation); Kauffman v. Truett, 771 A.2d 36 (Pa. Super. Ct. 2001); Department of Human Resources v. Cowan, 469 S.E.2d 384, 386 (Ga. Ct. App. 1996) (order terminating parental rights extinguishes support obligation, but voluntary surrender does not).

3. For a discussion of voluntary terminations, *see* Welsh, The Hon. Martin P. "Strategies for Obtaining Voluntary Consents in Termination of Parental Rights Cases." *ABA Child Law Practice* 21(2), April 2002, 17.

take the client seriously as a potential custodial resource, and helping create—not just preserve—a parent-child relationship.

For nonresident fathers, the child welfare system can be cold, unforgiving and filled with roadblocks. Without your zealous efforts, these clients may assume defeat and disappear from their children's lives. Representing a nonresident father is difficult work, but with careful planning and aggressive advocacy, these fathers can play an important role—big or small—in their children's lives. This benefits the father, his children, and society.

Endnotes

1. *See, e.g.,* M.V.S. v. M.D., 776 So. 2d 142, 148-50 (Ala. Civ. App. 1999) (failure of putative father to claim paternity under Ala. Code § 26-10C-1(f) results in irrevocable implied consent to adoption). *See, generally,* "Non-Resident Fathers, Paternal Kin and the Child Welfare System," National Quality Improvement Center on Non-Resident Fathers and the Child Welfare System, July 2007, 48, accessible at www.abanet.org/child/fathers/QICNRFLiteratureReview.pdf (hereinafter, "Non-Resident Fathers"). If the client is the child's "legal" father, you generally need not be concerned with later challenges to the client's paternity. But even if the client is the "legal" father, if the client was not living with the mother at or near the time of the child's birth, you may wish to ask him if he has any cause to believe that there may be a paternity challenge from a putative father.

2. The agency may have a copy of the child's birth certificate, especially if the family has been involved in the dependency process before. The mother (through her counsel) may be willing to give you a copy; if not, consider asking the court to order her to provide it.

3. *See, e.g.,* Fla. Stat. § 63.062(2), § 63.064(1); W. Va. Code § 48-22-301(b)(2), § 48-22-306. In most jurisdictions, such allegations are factors that the state may assert in proving parental unfitness, even if the state cannot assert them to challenge the nonresident father's standing.

4. *See* Smariga, Margaret. *Visitation with Infants and Toddlers in Foster Care: What Judges and Attorneys Need to Know.* Washington, D.C.: ABA Center on Children and the Law and Zero to Three, July 2007, accessible at www.abanet.org/child/policy-brief2.pdf.

5. In some jurisdictions, counsel for parents and children cannot speak directly to agency social workers without permission from agency counsel. Counsel must be aware of governing ethical rules and local practices when dealing with the agency social workers and supervisors.

6. *See, e.g.,* Cal. Welf. & Inst. Code § 362.1(a); In re Nicholas B., 106 Cal. Rptr. 2d 465 (Ct. App. 2001); N.Y. Family Ct. Act § 1030.

7. *See, e.g.,* Care and Protection of Isaac, 646 N.E.2d 1034, 1038-1039 (Mass. 1995).

8. In certain circumstances, counsel may wish to seek the appointment of a guardian ad litem (GAL) to report to the court on the advisability of increased visitation between father and child. This carries risks. An independent GAL may not agree that increased visitation serves the best interests of the child, and counsel, by moving for appointment of the GAL, may have only served to create an important adverse witness. Retaining an expert in child development or psychology—with court funds where appropriate—is usually preferable, provided counsel has the choice whether or not to present that expert's findings to the court.

9. *See, generally,* "Non-Resident Fathers," 2007, 50. Many jurisdictions require the agency to provide services to nonresident fathers. *See, e.g.,* In re Shaiesho O., 887 A.2d 415 (Conn. App. 2006); In re Asia Willis, 2002 WL 31114983 (Ohio Ct. App. 2002); Robin V. v. The Superior Court of Orange County, 39 Cal. Rptr. 2d 743 (Ct. App. 1995).

10. If the father has a history of abusing the mother or other women, direct him to programs designed to prevent further violence. For a discussion of services and strategies when working with batterers, *see* Goodmark, Leigh. "When a Parent is a Batterer: Understanding and Working with Abusive Fathers." *ABA Child Law Practice* 22(8), October 2003, 121.

11. *See* Chapter 1. "Advocating for the Constitutional Rights of Nonresident Fathers," by Vivek S. Sankaran.

12. Counsel must be familiar with the rules governing the admissibility of such evidence.

13. The resource may have his or her own counsel or may be unrepresented. Dealing with unrepresented parties—even friendly parties such as the nonresident father's kinship resource—presents many potential ethical traps. Counsel must be familiar with governing laws and rules for dealing with unrepresented parties.

14. *See* "How Do Social, Economic, and Cultural Factors Influence Fathers' Involvement with Their Children? A Summary of Key Research Findings." *Child Research Brief*, September 29, 1998. Available at www.childtrends.org.

15. *See, e.g.,* Mass. Gen. L. ch. 210, §§ 6C-6E (authorizing open adoption agreements); Adoption of Vito, 728 N.E.2d 292 (Mass. 2000) (authorizing courts to order postadoption contact between children and birth parents pursuant to their equitable powers).

16. *See, e.g.,* Mass. Gen. L. ch. 210, § 6D (specifying that the only remedy for breach of an open adoption agreement is specific performance, and that the parties have no right to appointment of counsel in enforcement litigation).

My Experiences with Child Welfare and the Legal System

In the following account, Shaine, a nonresident father, shares his experience in the child welfare system.

When my son, Cassady, was born in 2000, his mother and I were addicted to methamphetamines. Until Cassady was about three, I was in and out of his life as I struggled to get clean. In 2003, I went to my final treatment program, where I met my current wife, Shannon. We have both been clean ever since. I was ready to be in Cassady's life and began to see him and spend weekends together.

Unfortunately, as I was getting clean, Cassady's mom fell deeper into her addiction. In 2004, Cassady, his half brother, and his mom all tested positive for methamphetamines, which meant his mom was doing drugs around the children.

Choosing Foster Care over an Available Nonresident Father

DHS called to tell me that Cassady and his half-brother were being removed from their mother's home. They asked if I was willing to take Cassady and I said yes. But, when I arrived at DHS, the children were crying and Cassady's mother told the caseworker that she would rather have the children go to foster care together than split them up and give Cassady to me. DHS did as Cassady's mother requested. The children were in foster care for two months, after which they joined their mother in an inpatient treatment facility. I was only allowed to visit once a week. I had a demanding job two hours from where I lived and couldn't make the visits in time. I didn't see Cassady for the nine months while he was in the treatment facility with his mother.

In and Out of the System

DHS closed its case a few months after Cassady's mom left the treatment facility, but I heard that she had relapsed. I called DHS and they reopened the case. This time, DHS let her keep the children because her mother was in the home. They never considered me a placement option. I proved that I was clean and that I was working hard, but they didn't even look at me as an option.

"I told them that I wanted my son; I called every day begging for custody, but they put Cassady in foster care anyway."

A few months later, despite DHS's involvement, I learned that Cassady's mother was using drugs again and had not seen Cassady recently. Cassady and his mother both tested positive again. DHS informed me that they were going to put Cassady in foster care. DHS claimed that they wanted to keep Cassady in the same school, and that I wasn't a good placement option because I lived in a different city. I visited every weekend while he was back in foster care. I told them that I wanted my son; I called every day begging for custody, but they put Cassady in foster care anyway.

Going to Court

In June 2007, we went to court and Cassady was finally allowed to live with me. For the first year he was living with me, DHS was still trying to reunify him with his mom. They encouraged visits between Cassady and his mom, even though she tested positive for drugs. As she continued to use, she fell out of touch with Cassady and DHS. She has not seen Cassady in over a year. Since DHS lost contact with Cassady's mom, they stopped visiting my home; it is almost like they forgot about us since she disappeared.

Ongoing Court Battles

I worked hard to be a responsible, sober, working parent, but DHS was never on my side. I had to jump through hoops to be considered an option for my son, yet his mother kept getting chances and kept putting him in the same dangerous situations. Once I had Cassady, I received no support or services from DHS and I cannot get child support from his mother.

After DHS stopped visiting my home, I continued to struggle in the court system, trying to gain full custody of my son. I couldn't afford my own lawyer in this process, so I was appointed one. This experience has been negative and confusing. My lawyer rarely asks my opinion or what I hope to see happen during a hearing. If I do tell her something that I think should happen, it usually doesn't happen. In general, it feels like all decisions are made before we get to court.

Everyone always seemed worried about what Cassady's mom wanted, even though she got Cassady involved in the system. For me, it seems like DHS and the lawyers are just doing what's easiest for them, and everyone tells me different versions of what is happening. They have made me feel pressured to close the case, even though I don't have full custody yet. They know that it is a struggle for me because I have to miss work for every court date and every visit or evaluation, which can have a negative impact on my job.

I have a permanency hearing coming up. The judge is supposed to rule where Cassady will live. I have not been contacted by my attorney, the caseworker, the GAL, or anyone connected to the case and I am not sure where they stand. I don't think the court will award full custody to me, but I think DHS wants to close our case. If this happens, then both parents can continue to be involved in Cassady's life. I worry about sharing joint custody of Cassady, since his mom has repeatedly put him in dangerous situations. Despite this, DHS refuses to terminate her rights and won't help me get full custody. I think I have proved myself to be a good, safe parent, so it does not make sense to me why they won't support my position.

New Beginnings

Since Cassady has been with me, he is clean and healthy. He went from being a child who couldn't count to 10 to a second grader who reads at a fifth grade level. He is involved in wrestling and baseball. My wife and I have overcome our own struggles with addiction to do what is best for our family. We are raising four other boys and know that we are the best, safest place for Cassady. We hope that DHS and the court system will recognize that soon.

—*Ellen Kinney, American Humane Association*

Lessons Learned for Lawyers Representing Nonresident Fathers

This is the true story of a dad who struggled through the child welfare system to gain custody of his child. He faced many roadblocks along the way, including his substance abuse problems. But, many of these barriers arose from poor advocacy, institutional biases, and resistance by professionals to properly engage Shaine early in the child welfare case. As a lawyer for a nonresident father, you can learn from Shaine's story. Avoid years of litigation and oversight that can harm the father and his child by taking these steps.

1. **Make your case early.** Shaine had an opportunity to gain temporary custody of his son before he was placed in foster care. But, without advocacy and a chance to express his position, he lost custody of his child for a long period.

2. **Make sure visitation is set up in a way that ensures your client's participation.** In Shaine's case, visitation was not feasible because it was arranged without regard for his work schedule. He wanted to see his child, but wasn't given a fair chance to do so for almost a year.

3. **Encourage the court and agency to consider your client a viable placement option.** Offer proof of his capacity to parent and willingness to engage in necessary services. Shaine begged the agency to consider him as a placement option, but the agency didn't for a long time, causing his child to enter the foster care system unnecessarily. He needed, but didn't get, strong advocacy in and out of court and reliable proof to show his fitness.

4. **Ensure your father client receives supportive services to transition his child into his home.** Although Shaine successfully gained custody of his child, he did not receive support from the agency that could have helped him navigate being a first-time custodial parent to a child who had been through the foster care system and regularly exposed to drugs.

5. **Understand how your jurisdiction handles the intersection between child welfare and other family law matters.** Shaine has struggled for years to gain full custody of his child through proceedings outside the child welfare case and with little legal help. Attorneys for fathers should be aware of low-cost or free legal aid programs in their area where they can refer their father clients. (See the *ABA Directory of Pro Bono Programs*, available at www.abanet.org/legalservices/probono/directory.html#.)

6. **Establish a relationship with your client and maintain regular contact.** Shaine is ready to prepare for an important upcoming hearing in his child's case but has not been able to contact his counsel to share his goals and strategize. He is ready to work toward his goal of full custody but lacks an established relationship with his advocate to do so.

—Jessica Kendall, ABA Center on Children and the Law

CHAPTER FIVE

Engaging Fathers in the Child Protection Process: The Judicial Role

Judge Leonard P. Edwards (ret.)

CHECKLIST

Engaging Fathers in the Child Protection Process: The Judicial Role

Identify and locate all possible fathers early.

➤ Question the mother under oath regarding the identity of the father.

➤ Determine where the father can be located by questioning parties about his whereabouts.

➤ Order the social worker to follow up on information gained from the court hearing.

➤ Revisit the question of identity and location of the father at all subsequent court hearings.

Complete paternity testing as soon as possible.

➤ When a potential father comes to court, let him know the court is pleased that he has appeared because he is an important person in the child's life.

➤ Let him know that once his paternity is established, he will be treated as a parent in all subsequent court proceedings.

➤ Ensure testing costs are at state expense unless the father has means to pay.

Appoint counsel for the father.

➤ Appoint counsel as soon as paternity is established, with the possibility of reimbursement considering his financial means.

Engage fathers in the child protection case.

➤ Insist that social workers use good faith efforts to identify, locate, and support fathers throughout the case.

➤ Use the "no reasonable efforts" finding if necessary to ensure father engagement.

➤ Make it clear that the father may be a placement possibility for the child.

➤ Encourage developing community-based services that meet the needs of fathers, like parenting classes for fathers, fathers mentoring fathers, and other gender-specific programs.

Involve paternal relatives in the case.

➤ Identify the father's extended family and ensure they know about the legal proceedings and that they will be considered as possible placements if necessary.

➤ Permit the extended family to participate in group decision-making processes, visitation, and court hearings, where appropriate.

Address domestic violence issues.

➤ Determine if the father is a danger to the mother or to the child and consider appropriate protective orders.

Download this and other checklists at **www.fatherhoodqic.org/checklists**

Nonresident fathers rarely appear in child welfare proceedings.[1] Several reasons stand out: the father is hard to locate, the mother is ambivalent about engaging the father, the caseworker devalues fathers, and the father feels outside the process and does not want to participate. The list goes on.[2]

As a judge presiding over child welfare cases, you have the power to remove barriers and promote fathers' involvement in child welfare legal proceedings. Fathers are important to the child and to the legal process[3] and you play a critical role in engaging them. This chapter explores:

- why it is important to engage fathers in the child welfare process;
- the judge's role in determining who the father is and in establishing paternity;
- the judge's role in monitoring agency actions to identify, locate, notify, and support the father;
- the judge's role in engaging fathers and their families in the child welfare process, both in and out of court; and
- safety considerations for the mother and child if the father presents dangers to one or both.

Making Father Engagement a Priority

Fathers need to be engaged in the lives of their children[4] unless they pose a threat of harm. In the absence of any risk of harm, judges must take steps to ensure fathers participate in the court process.[5] Engaging fathers in the child welfare case and legal proceedings is important for several reasons:

- **Protects the father's legal rights.** The father has a legal right to participate in the proceedings. If the court process does not include the father, in some states he may be able to attack the proceedings. The father's "late arrival" in the proceedings can affect the outcome for the child and delay permanency.[6] Sometimes the child welfare process must start over to give the father a fair opportunity to reunify with his child. If the father was never notified of the proceedings, even an adoption could be overturned.[7]

- **Promotes children's social well-being and healthy development.** Research reveals that children have better outcomes when two parents are involved with their upbringing.[8] A father's presence can give the child a sense of belonging to a complete family. A father can help the child understand who he is and how he fits into the social scheme of his family and the world around him.

- **Promotes family connections.** The father's family provides an additional resource for the child socially, emotionally, and financially. The father's family, on average, will provide the child with one-half of his or her relatives. Studies show that this can mean scores if not hundreds of potential relative connections.[9]

- **Provides financial resources for the child.** A father can bring financial support directly or through child support to the caretaker.[10] The father may also provide health and dental insurance. The father's extended family also offers opportunities for economic support.

Identifying Fathers and Determining Paternity

The father is often viewed as the male biological parent of a child. But whether he will be acknowledged by the law as a father entitled to all of the legal rights and protections given to the mother will be determined by other factors such as:
- Was he married to the mother at the time of conception?
- If not, did he acknowledge that he is the father of the child? When did he do so?
- Was he present at the birth of the child?
- Did he acknowledge paternity at the hospital or place his name on the birth certificate?
- Did he live with and support the child after birth?
- Did he attempt to have contact with and support the child after birth? Was he prevented from doing so?
- Is there more than one person claiming to be the father?
- Did he register on a paternity registry?

Depending on state law and answers to the above questions, biological fathers in some jurisdictions may find they have fewer rights than in others. It is your role to sort this out and declare who the father is and his legal status regarding the child before the court. Accomplishing this involves aggressively pursuing paternity from the outset of the case.[11]

Questioning the caseworker

Sometimes the information collected by the caseworker before the initial hearing will be incomplete regarding the identity, location, and legal status of the father. Always ask the caseworker whether she has had contact with anyone claiming to be the father of the child. If so, follow up by asking if the caseworker offered paternity testing and informed him of the court proceedings and his right to participate.

Questioning the mother

Obtain as much information from the mother as possible by questioning her under oath. When trying to identify and locate a father with a reluctant mother, you will need to ask probing questions. The following courtroom exchange typifies the judge's role in determining the identity and location of the father from a reluctant mother.

> **Judge:** Good morning, Ms. Jones. Thank you for coming to court today. As you know we are here today regarding the legal proceedings involving your child. I have several questions I must ask you at the outset. They are required by law. They are so important that I am going to ask you to raise your right hand and give an oath that you will tell the truth (oath administered). First, are you married?
>
> **Mother:** No.
>
> **Judge:** Have you ever been married?
>
> **Mother:** Yes, but I think we are divorced. At least, he said he was going to get a divorce. I haven't seen him for years.
>
> **Judge:** What is that person's name?
>
> **Mother:** Jack Williams.
>
> **Judge:** How can we contact him?
>
> **Mother:** I have his address because the child support people have been getting him to pay support for the past few months.
>
> **Judge:** Will you please give that information to the social worker after court?[12]
>
> **Mother:** Alright.
>
> **Judge:** Who is the father of your newborn son, Charlie?
>
> **Mother:** I don't know.
>
> **Judge:** Ms. Jones, it is necessary that I know who the father is. These are important legal proceedings and you must answer my questions. Who is Charlie's father?
>
> **Mother:** I only met him once.

Judge: Where did you meet him?

Mother: In a bar.

Judge: What is the name of the bar?

Mother: I forget.

Judge: Where is the bar?

Mother: It's on the corner of 4th and Washington, downtown.

Judge: What did you call him when you met him?

Mother: He just went by "Big Al."

Judge: Did you see him there more than once?

Mother: Yeah, he hangs out there.

Judge: Did he say where he worked?

Mother: No.

Judge: Did he say where he lived?

Mother: No.

Judge: Have you seen him lately?

Mother: Once in a while.

Judge: Have you told him about Charlie?

Mother: I may have told him.

Judge: Was he present at the birth of the baby?

Mother: No way!!

Judge: Has he ever seen the baby?

Mother: No way, I wouldn't let him near the baby.

Judge: Did he ever see you when you were pregnant?

Mother: I don't remember.

Judge: Did he ever talk about his family?

Mother: I don't remember.

Judge: Ms. Jones…this is very important. Did he tell you about his family?

Mother: He said he lived with his mother and aunt.

Judge: Could you show the social worker or your lawyer where the bar is?

Mother: I guess so.

Judge: Could you point out Big Al to them if you saw him?

Mother: I guess so, but you have to watch out, as I hear he is dangerous.

Judge: Thank you, Ms. Jones. Ms. Tompkins (the caseworker), did you hear the answers that Ms. Jones gave? I order you to follow up on that information. Moreover, I order you to continue this search as long as this child's case is before the court.

Your stature as the judge is such that answers are likely to be forthcoming, answers that may not be revealed to a caseworker or even to a lawyer. It takes extra time for judicial questioning, but the results are well worth it.

Ordering agency follow up

Order the agency to follow up on the information disclosed by the mother, search for the father, and give him notice of the proceedings. Follow up on the agency's progress at subsequent hearings.

Questioning potential fathers directly

Sometimes a man claiming to be the father will appear at the courthouse. Be sure the person responsible for bringing parties into the courtroom (e.g., bailiff or other court officer) informs you of all parties who wish to be present in the courtroom. Decide who will be permitted to be present and for what portion of proceedings. Question a potential father directly about his relationship to the mother, relationship to child, desire to be a father, and his efforts to establish a relationship with the child. If the man may be the father, take steps to protect his rights, such as ordering the agency to arrange for and pay for paternity testing; setting a date for paternity test results; and appointing counsel. Consider the following exchange:

Judge: Good morning. What is your name?

Father: Good morning, Judge. I'm John Soto and I'm the father of the child, little Harry.

Judge: Well, I am going to ask you some important questions about your relationship to Ms. Rivera and the child, little Harry. Would you please stand while my clerk administers the oath? (oath administered) Are you married to the mother, Ms. Rivera?

Father: No sir, I'm not, but I know he's my son.

Judge: Are you living with Ms. Rivera?

Father: No sir, she and I had a falling out and she won't talk to me, and she wouldn't let me see the boy.

Judge: Were you present when the baby was born a few months ago.

Father: I wanted to be, but she wouldn't tell me where the hospital was.

Judge: Do you want to be a father to this child?

Father: I sure do and so does my family. My mother and father and a sister are outside the courtroom and they want to visit with the child also. My sister would love to have the child live with her, if he can't return to his mother's care or live with me.

Judge: Ms. Rivera, do you believe that Mr. Soto is Harry's biological father?

Mother: I guess so, judge.

Judge: Madam Social Worker, I order you to arrange for DNA testing to determine if Mr. Soto is the biological father of the child. I want that completed as soon as possible at department expense[13] with the results returned to court in 14 days.[14] Furthermore, in light of the financial affidavit that Mr. Soto has filled out I am appointing Mr. William Frank to represent Mr. Soto through these proceedings. My court attendant will give you Mr. Frank's telephone number, Mr. Soto.

There could be different answers and outcomes to this scenario, but the judge is demonstrating the importance of determining paternity at the earliest possible stage. If the father had shown ambivalence and decided he did not want to participate in the proceedings, the judge might have just let him walk out.

Protecting the legal rights of alleged fathers

Unfortunately, some state statutes create obstacles for nonresident fathers including those who might be interested in connecting with their children and participating in child welfare proceedings. These statutes may require the father to file a legal action to determine his paternity, register in a paternity registry, or take other independent action to have the right to receive notice and participate in the proceedings.[15]

One troubling situation involves a man the mother claims is the father to whom she is not married and who otherwise would not qualify as a putative or

■ Views from the Bench: Engaging Fathers

While little has been written about engaging fathers from a judicial perspective, juvenile and family court judges, child support commissioners, and other judicial officers have thought a great deal about this issue. Interviews with judicial officers from four different jurisdictions revealed several themes.

➤ **Encourage the agency to locate the father early:** Regularly ask about the father's whereabouts and hold the agency accountable for not looking hard enough and for not offering appropriate reunification services. Insist that social workers take seriously their role in questioning the mother about the identity and location of the father. Ensure the intake officer requires the father's information on the petition so the social worker gets in the habit of securing that information.

➤ **Consider the father as a resource:** Make it clear that the father should be considered for placement, if not immediately, then sometime soon. Encourage and facilitate regular visits between the father and child. Hold the agency accountable for failing to provide fathers with meaningful reunification services.

➤ **Engage fathers in the court process:** Tell them that "anyone can be a father, but it takes dedication to be a daddy." Share studies that show that children fare better if both parents are involved in their lives. Explain to the parties that just because a father is nonresident it does not mean he is unfit. Permit appearances by phone to accommodate work schedules, transportation problems, incarceration or other conflicts fathers may have. Order paternity testing if necessary. Offer evaluations, family contact, treatment, and transportation assistance.

➤ **Encourage interagency collaborations:** Coordinate with parent representation offices to appoint counsel for indigent fathers. Facilitate the development of protocols with child support enforcement whereby the father's child support obligation can be suspended if he has custody under a juvenile court order.

➤ **Use training to educate the court system about the importance of engaging fathers:** This includes not only child welfare cases, but all cases involving children where engaging fathers is a problem (e.g., delinquency, child support).

Sources:

These tips were drawn from interviews with: Commissioner Marilyn Kading Martinez, Los Angeles County Juvenile Court; Judge Stephen Rubin, Pima County, Arizona, Juvenile Court; Commissioner John Schroeder, Santa Clara County Child Support Commissioner; Judge Constance Cohen, Juvenile Court Judge, Des Moines, Iowa.

presumed father under the Uniform Parentage Act.[16] In many states this person is called an alleged father. Best practice is for the court to order that he be notified of the proceedings. In some jurisdictions, the court will immediately appoint counsel to represent him and help locate and advise him of his rights.[17] Most states will not appoint counsel unless paternity is established, while some states rarely or never appoint counsel for a father or mother at any stage of the proceedings.[18]

Devote time to determining whether an alleged father is the biological father of the child. Many children are born out-of-wedlock,[19] and many children in child welfare proceedings come from unmarried parents. These children did not choose their parents or their parents' marital status. To punish them for their parents' behaviors is wrong. It is also unconstitutional.[20] These children deserve the same level of advocacy and assistance connecting to and reunifying with family as children of married parents.

The father who appears and asks for custody raises complex issues. Assuming that he is a fit parent, should the court place the child with him and dismiss the case? That would be the result had the mother died since he would be the child's surviving parent. Should the court give no preference to the father at all and simply use a "best interests" test to determine custody? Should the court place the child with the father, maintain the child under court supervision, and give the mother an opportunity to use services to reunify with her child? States have responded to these issues in different ways both through statutes and appellate decisions.[21]

Monitoring Agency Actions

Do not assume the child welfare agency is doing all it can to identify, locate, notify, and support the father in child welfare proceedings. The Adoption Assistance and Child Welfare Act of 1980[22] requires court oversight of agency actions in child welfare cases. Further, the Child and Family Service Reviews (CFSRs) assess each child welfare agency on:

1) whether they made concerted efforts to involve *parents* in the case-planning process on an ongoing basis;

2) whether the caseworker had frequent and high quality meetings with the *parents*; and

3) whether the caseworker demonstrated concerted efforts to provide visits of sufficient quantity and quality to promote continuity in the child's relationship with the *parents* and siblings[23] (emphasis added).

The CFSR assessments require the caseworker to work with both parents throughout the time a child's case is before the court. These federal laws and guidelines clarify the agency's responsibilities and the court's role in monitoring agency compliance. Within the context of each case, the court can specify what it expects of the agency and hold it accountable.[24]

Assessing the agency's actions

At the shelter care hearing,[25] ask what actions the agency has taken to identify and locate the father.[26] Has the agency's caseworker:

- asked the mother about the identity and location of the father?
- used any search technology such as the child support locater to locate the father?
- asked the mother's relatives about the father and his relatives?
- asked the mother about the identity and location of any of the father's relatives?
- used family-finding technology to identify the father's relatives?[27]
- contacted any of the father's relatives concerning his location?
- checked with local jail or state prison representatives (or prisoner locator Web sites) to determine if the father is incarcerated? (See Chapter 4, *Locating Your Client: A Checklist* box.)
- checked with probation or parole authorities to determine if the father is on probation or parole?
- talked with the child or the child's siblings about contact with the father or father's relatives?

At interim review hearings, address the caseworker's efforts to identify and locate the father and review relevant court reports. If the caseworker has failed to follow through, consider making a finding of "no reasonable efforts" since identifying the father can prevent foster care placements.[28]

Ensuring the father is notified

Notifying the father that legal proceedings have commenced is another critical stage in child welfare cases. State statutes differ on the type of notice required before the court can proceed. Some states do not require the state (agency) to give an unmarried father notice of child welfare proceedings, or only require notice when that person has taken specific steps such as entering his name in a paternity registry.[29] Illinois, on the other hand, includes unmarried fathers in the definition of parent and requires personal service when the case starts.[30] Notifying the father is so important that Illinois gives him the right to demand a shelter care rehearing when he finally appears.[31] Only after extensive efforts can the agency use substituted service, namely publication, to notify the father.[32] This commitment to engaging the father is a best practice that other state legislatures should emulate.

Ordering DNA testing to establish paternity

When ordering DNA or other testing to determine paternity, make your expectations known regarding payment for the test—the Title IV-D agency or the child welfare agency, depending on which can accomplish the DNA testing more quickly or at the lowest cost. These are issues that impact the child's best interests as well as the timeliness of the court process, already under strict ASFA guidelines. If there is any question about the agency's follow through, hold an interim review to check on the progress of the testing.

Ensuring visits begin once paternity is established

Once paternity is established, visitation should begin immediately unless there is reason to believe such contact would harm the child.[33] The agency should not wait for weeks or months to return to court to start that visitation. Ensure visits begin promptly by making an order for visitation contingent upon the paternity finding without requiring a return to court. The agency should also consider permitting the father's relatives to participate with the father in visits. Relatives may help the father develop a positive relationship with his child.

Ensuring the agency provides services to the father

Make it clear that you expect the agency to offer the father services once paternity is established. Since some fathers ask for service referrals before paternity is determined, the court should encourage the agency to permit this to occur without requiring a return to court.

Court-Engagement Strategies

Engaging fathers in the child welfare process involves strategic thinking and planning. For the father who enthusiastically comes to court asking to fully engage in his child's life, participate in services, and attend all court hearings, there is little the court needs to do. The enthusiastic father, however, is the exception. More often the father is ambivalent about participating in the case, his relationship to the mother, and coming to court. Moreover, he may worry about getting involved

Iowa's Approach to Engaging Fathers

Iowa has taken steps to engage fathers in the child welfare process. Iowa's success comes despite a statutory scheme that treats nonresident fathers as little more than an intervenor.[1] According to Judge Constance Cohen, the judiciary does its best to provide notice, counsel, and services to fathers promptly. Engagement efforts cut across the entire dependency process in Iowa and include:[2]

➤ The public defender's office appoints counsel, subject to the filing of a financial affidavit, so all identified parents have legal representation at the first hearing.

➤ At expanded preliminary hearings held within five days of removal,[3] the court orders paternity testing if necessary, and offers evaluations, family contact, treatment, transportation assistance, and other frontloaded services.

➤ Iowa courts provide parents handbooks at the first hearing to help them understand the nature of the proceedings.

➤ Judges present fathers with a "now or never" proposition, making it clear that full involvement is expected and that it may be too late if they wait for the mother to fail to try to assume custody.

➤ Fathers may participate by phone to accommodate work schedules, transportation problems, incarceration, and other barriers to personal presence at court hearings.

➤ Courts may find compelling reasons to maintain a father's legal rights beyond 15 months in cases in which the mother has purposefully frustrated the father's efforts to locate and become involved with the child.

➤ In cases involving siblings with different fathers where the mother is not a possible placement but one father can take custody of some or all of the children, expedited foster care licensing may be explored to keep the siblings together.

➤ The Parent Partners program works with parents who have successfully navigated the system to mentor parents who are new to the system. Fathers, in particular, benefit from these mentor relationships.

➤ Iowa's Fatherhood Initiative developed by the court and community supports fathers and provides educational tools.

➤ A Zero-to-Three project has made special efforts to motivate fathers to participate in all aspects of a case. It offers attachment assessments, dyadic therapy, family contact, and other frontloaded services.[4]

➤ A statewide protocol provides that a child support payor's obligation may be suspended if he has custody under a juvenile court order. This creates an economic incentive for the father to ask for custody.

Sources:

1. "A parent without custody may petition the court to be made a party to proceedings under this division. Iowa Code § 232.91(1).

2. E-mail correspondence from Judge Constance Cohen, Juvenile Court Judge, Des Moines, Iowa. Copy available from the author.

3. The local rule mandates the hearing take place within 10 days, but local practice is for the hearing to take place in five days, again because of the expedited nature of the proceedings.

4. Phone conversations with Judge Constance Cohen and Judy Norris, director of the Zero to Three project.

in legal proceedings for reasons relating to his immigration status, criminal history, concerns about child support, or poor relationships with the caseworkers or lawyers.

Treating fathers with respect

When the father appears in court, treat him with respect, acknowledging his importance to the legal proceedings and to the child.[34] Simple courtesies can make the difference between a positive and negative court experience for the father. Take time to explain such issues as the nature of the proceedings, the importance of fathers, permanency issues and timelines, the father's legal rights, and the potential role of the father's family for the child.

Judge: Good morning Mr. Smith. How are you today?

Mr. Smith: Fine thanks, Judge. Say, just why am I here today?

Judge: Mr. Smith, I have a number of important questions to ask you today. Please stand and raise your right hand so that my clerk can administer the oath (oath administered). Mr. Smith, Miss Francis says that you are the father of her baby boy, Ricky. There are legal proceedings involving Ricky, and, if you are the father, you have a right to participate in those proceedings. Is it possible you are the father?

Mr. Smith: Well, I don't know judge. Miss Francis has a lot of boyfriends, and I'm not married to her, you know.

Judge: Well she seems pretty sure that you are the father. That's great news isn't it!

Mr. Smith: I don't rightly know, Judge.

Judge: Being a father is a wonderful event. I want to offer my congratulations.

Mr. Smith: Thanks, Judge, but I'd like to be sure. Could I get some testing done to make certain that I'm the father?

Judge: Certainly, Mr. Jones. The caseworker will arrange for DNA testing this week. Will you go to the testing center when she tells you the date?

Mr. Smith: I guess so.

Judge: Have you told your parents about Ricky?

Mr. Smith: I did mention it to my mother.

Judge: And was she happy with the news?

Mr. Smith: Yeah, she was pretty excited.

Judge: As soon as the testing is completed, would you like to have visits with Ricky?

Mr. Smith: Sure, I guess.

Judge: Would you like it if your mother was also able to visit?

Mr. Smith: Sure, I guess. I know she would like it.

Judge: The caseworker can refer you to a class for new fathers where you could meet with other young men to discuss what it means to be a father and how to care for your child. Would you like to participate in that class?

Mr. Smith: Sure, if I'm the father, I'll do it.

Judge: You understand that if I find you to be Ricky's father, I will make the class a part of your case plan. So you will be getting a head start if you get going now.

Mr. Smith: I understand, Judge.

Judge: Would you like a picture of Ricky?

Mr. Smith: Yes, that would be nice.

Judge: Once the testing is complete, the caseworker will provide you with one. I want you to return to court in 10 days. I will appoint you a lawyer once the paternity testing is complete and you are proven to be the father. Then there will be another hearing in two weeks. You have a right to appear at that hearing and all hearings thereafter.

Removing barriers to participation

Identify and remove barriers to the father's participation and encourage him to become involved with his child. The barriers include anything that makes it more difficult for the father to play a role in his child's life. For example, ask whether the father has transportation to and from the facility that will perform the DNA testing, to court proceedings, to the site for visitation, and to the location of services. Ensure that there are language interpreters for non-English speaking fathers and that those interpreters are available at all critical events in the case. Also determine whether the father's relatives want to be involved in the child's life.

Appointing qualified counsel

Appointing counsel for the father is critical to his involvement in the court process. Counsel can inform the court about problems the father is experiencing that otherwise would escape the court's notice. Counsel can facilitate communication between the father and the caseworker and can ensure the father's rights are upheld.

There is no constitutional right to counsel for indigent parents in child welfare cases.[35] State laws and practices vary regarding appointing counsel for indigent parents. A 1998 survey found:

- Thirty-nine states provide that counsel be appointed for indigent parents.
- Six states include provisions that counsel be appointed for parents in all child welfare proceedings.
- Three states provide only for the appointment of counsel for parents in termination of parental rights cases.
- Three states do not provide explicitly for the appointment of counsel in statute.[36]

Seventy-eight percent of the survey respondents reported that counsel is appointed at some point during a child welfare case, while 11% of the respondents said that counsel for parents is generally not appointed.[37] The survey also found that appointed parents' counsel is often inadequate for three reasons:

1) inadequate time to prepare;
2) inadequate time, resources, and compensation to adequately represent clients; and
3) tension between zealously representing parent clients and "core concepts" of morality [that] dictate care and concern for the abused child.[38]

Barriers to Engaging Fathers

Understanding why fathers are important in child welfare cases is the first step to fully engaging them in the legal process. If the child welfare system does not have a role for fathers, then developing engagement strategies wastes time. Common barriers to engaging fathers are:

➤ **Mothers' reluctance to reveal name or location of father.**[1] Many mothers have had violent or unhealthy episodes with the father. Others have a new romantic relationship and want to forget about their child's biological father. Some may want to protect him from involvement with the court. Still others are reluctant to bring the current abuse or neglect episode to the attention of the father, fearing he will ask for custody.[2]

➤ **Caseworkers' ambivalence about finding fathers.**[3] Some caseworkers have had negative experiences with fathers and suspect that the father is not interested in the child. Others fear that bringing the father into the child welfare case may introduce another abusive person or increase conflict between the parents.[4] Caseworkers know that engaging fathers will result in more work, will be more costly to the agency, and find that working with mothers alone is easier.[5]

➤ **Legal system's failure to give priority to locating or engaging fathers**, particularly if the father is not married to the mother, is incarcerated, or has a violent or criminal history.[6]

(For further discussion of barriers to father engagement, see *Chapter 2, Understanding Male Help-Seeking Behaviors.*)

Sources:

1. *See, e.g.,* G.P. v Florida, 842 So. 2d. 1059 (Fla. Dist. Ct. App. 2003) (holding mother had a constitutional privacy right to withhold name of her child's father).

2. Harris, L. "Involving Nonresident Fathers in Dependency Cases: New Efforts, New Problems, New Solutions." *Journal of Law & Family Studies* 9(2), 2007, 299-397.

3. Malm, K., J. Murray and R. Geen. *What about the Dads? Child Welfare Agencies' Efforts to Identify, Locate and Involve Nonresident Fathers.* Washington, D.C.: U.S. Department of Health and Human Services, Office of the Assistant Secretary of Planning and Evaluation, 2006, ix, 85-86.

4. Ibid., 25.

5. *See* Rosenberg, J. and W.B. Wilcox. *The Importance of Fathers in the Healthy Development of Children.* Washington, D.C.: U.S. Department of Health & Human Services, 2006, 33.

6. National Child Welfare Resource Center for Family-Centered Practice. "Father Involvement in Child Welfare: Estrangement and Reconciliation." Washington, D.C.: U.S. Department of Health and Human Services, ACYF, Children's Bureau, Summer 2002, 1-2.

The survey shows that representation for indigent parents is not provided in all states, and when it is provided it is often inadequate. Appointing counsel for nonresident fathers occurs less frequently than for mothers and presumed (putative) fathers. For adequate counsel to be appointed for nonresident fathers, standards of representation must be raised. Some jurisdictions, such as the District of Columbia, already set high standards by appointing counsel for all fathers.

The court should also require counsel to participate in training focused on representing fathers.[39] Some courts require all appointed lawyers to complete trainings and observe and participate in court proceedings before becoming eligible for court appointment.[40] Such requirements ensure the availability of an experienced panel of lawyers for representation of parents, and particularly fathers, in child welfare cases.[41]

Encouraging the father

Encourage the father to take pride in his new status as father and help him identify the positive aspects of being a father. These include visiting, sharing with other family members, exchanging photos, participating in doctor visits, and more. Congratulate the father, reminding him that this is a major societal and family event. This encouragement can come from any male in the courtroom:

Judge: You know I am a father, too.

Father: Oh?

Judge: Yes, having a son/daughter has been one of most important parts of my life. There are so many things we do together. You have a great deal to look forward to as a father.[42]

Consider asking the father if he had a relationship with his own father. Depending on the answer, you might follow up with, "Would you like to have a good relationship with your child?" If the answer is yes, offer to help with that. If the father works, compliment him and offer praise for his role in supporting his child and tell him how important economic support is to the child's well-being.[43]

The court can also present barriers to engagement by making it difficult for the father to visit, come to court, or engage in services. Some courts show a bias towards alleged fathers that harms the father and child.[44] Without appellate court oversight some trial courts will continue to provide only minimal due process or support for fathers.

Identifying and Engaging the Extended Family

Extended family can help engage fathers with their children. The young father may not understand the importance of a new family member to other family members and to the family unit. Other family members—grandparents, aunts, uncles, and siblings—understand how important a new family member is, particularly a baby. They will want to be a part of the baby's care and for the baby to remain in the family. Moreover, they will likely influence the father more than any professional in the child welfare system.[45] Parents, siblings, and other relatives may be able to hold the father accountable for his behavior and ensure he participates in the legal proceedings.

Young fathers can be uncomfortable with infants. Typically they do not know how to play with or comfort them. Extended family members can help the father learn how to relate to and feel more comfortable with his child, and make him understand how important this new addition to the family is to everyone. A father visiting with an infant by himself may have a difficult experience and give up his efforts to be involved in his child's life. A father visiting with a relative sees the child in the hands of a more skilled family member and learns how to be a better father.

As the judge, you can play an important role in making the extended family a part of the child welfare case. Insist that extended family be told of the legal proceedings, invited to court, and included in visitation arrangements so that they can help engage the father in his child's life.

Identifying and engaging relatives is sound policy. It also is the law in many states and is emphasized in recent federal legislation.[46] The Fostering Connections to Success and Increasing Adoptions Act stresses the identification of extended family, the engagement of relatives, and the preference for consideration of relatives. There are also more than 23 "relative preference" states—states with statutes that give preference to relatives over nonrelatives when a child is removed from parental care and placed out of home. This is also the practice in some states without relative preference statutes. It is good caseworker practice to identify and work with extended family members. Usually these relatives know the child, which makes placement with them less traumatic to the child. They also share DNA with the child, making it likely that they will treat the child with love and will work to make the child's environment family-like. Some research shows that relative placements are safer than nonrelative placements.[47] It is also well established that relatives provide a significant percentage of care for children placed out of home.[48]

Protecting the Safety of the Mother and Child

Do not assume the father in the child welfare case is harmless or a positive influence in the child's life. He may be dangerous, violent, a substance abuser, or have sexual or mental health problems. You will need good information about the father to make decisions about his contact with the child and with the mother. Be prepared to restrict contact, if necessary, and have domestic violence protocols and practices in place that address when mediation or other group decision-making processes should be used.[49]

However, just because the father is violent or dangerous does not mean his entire family is to be avoided. Some people subscribe to the maxim that "the apple does not fall from the tree," meaning that if the father is dangerous, the entire family must be dangerous. Group decision-making practices often uncover some solid, stable members in a family, no matter how violent or dangerous one or more members may be.

Assuming the father is a danger, if a family member steps forward to receive a child into their home, find out whether the family member understands what the father has done and is willing to protect the child from the father in the future. This issue is challenging for family members because they often love the father and cannot accept that he has done or may do something abusive towards the child. Weigh these considerations when making a placement decision.

Using Nonadversarial Processes

The adversarial court process does not build relationships, strengthen families, or encourage participation by fathers or other family members.[50] Fathers (and most family members) are intimidated by the adversarial process and most do not want to come to court and have a trial. As a result, they either do not attend or sit silently in child welfare proceedings. The courtroom does not permit the parent to speak freely. Instead, any expressions are restricted by the rules of evidence and time restrictions. An important strategy for the child welfare system is to have opportunities outside of court to resolve matters, preferably in a confidential setting where family members can work with others to address the needs of their child.[51]

Group decision making

Encourage the agency to use group decision-making processes that bring together family members, friends, and professionals to address issues relating to the child.[52]

Family members work together to plan for the future of their children. Resources within the family and close friends are identified, family members help make it possible for the child to remain with relatives, and fathers see that they are a part of a greater family that wants to raise its children. The father also sees that he has a part to play in the family, and that he is important to his child. Every effort should be made to include fathers in group decision making. In North San Diego County, for example, the agency will not convene a team decision-making meeting (TDM) without the father, believing his involvement and the involvement of his family almost always benefits the child.[53]

Mediation

Many child welfare courts across the country have started mediation programs with great success.[54] Family members prefer mediation to the court process because they feel that they are heard (for the first time) and they can work with others to fashion a result with which everyone agrees.[55] If your jurisdiction lacks a child welfare mediation program, encourage your court administration to start one.

Ensuring Quality Father-Child Visits

Pay special attention to visitation between children and their fathers. Frequency, duration, location, and environment (including who else is present) can make the difference between effective visitation that builds a relationship and visitation that discourages the father.[56] Visitation once a month or once a week is insufficient to build a relationship. Meeting for 30 minutes is not long enough to engage father and child. Meeting in a room by oneself is also not conducive to strengthening a relationship. Insist that visitation take place frequently, that it last at least an hour (longer is preferable), that it occur in a family-like setting, and that others (such as relatives or supportive foster parents) are permitted to attend with the father.[57]

Some fathers will benefit from support or coaching before or during visits. Sophisticated supports and techniques for visiting exist to enhance parenting skills during visitation. The agency and the judge should consider referring fathers to "visit coaching" to make visits as positive as possible.[58] These coaching services prepare fathers to meet children they have not seen or had much contact with, and are particularly useful for incarcerated fathers.[59]

Visitation should be expanded to include other locations and events rather than just time at a visitation center.[60] For example, make orders that permit fathers to get notice of and to participate in all well-baby doctor visits as well as the child's other appointments. For the school-aged child, this includes parent-teacher conferences and sporting or cultural events in which the child participates. Church-based events such as baptisms, Sunday school, and other occasions also offer opportunities for meaningful father-child contact.

Ensuring Fathers Receive Parenting Services

Many fathers need help learning how to be a father, particularly young fathers. Be prepared to refer the father to services that will provide basic information about child development and skill development for parents.[61] Most jurisdictions offer parenting classes, and some offer parenting classes that focus on infants. The most useful classes bring together fathers and their children so the father can work and play with the child in the context of the parenting class.[62] Also useful are programs that bring new fathers together to address their unique needs.[63] Some communities have mentoring programs that match experienced fathers with new fathers so that one can learn from the other.

Pressing for father-specific services

Know what services are available in your community. Community-based organizations such as the YMCA often provide services for fathers. If no appropriate services exist, explore how they might be developed. Excellent service models exist around the country.[64] If no services specific to fathers exist, ask the agency to develop them. You may decide that a parenting class or a parenting class for fathers is a reasonable service for the community to provide and insist that the agency create one. Failure to do so would result in a "no reasonable efforts" finding.[65]

Handling reluctant fathers

Some fathers will balk at the idea that they should participate in any services. The father may say something like "[s]he was the one who neglected my child. Why should I have to do anything?" Be prepared to discuss the importance and value of the service being offered. When speaking to a father about services, one judge suggests advising: "You are a father. Now you need to learn how to be a daddy."[66]

Working with Incarcerated Fathers

Many foster children have parents in jail or prison. Of this population there are far more incarcerated fathers than mothers.[67] Some of these fathers are "alleged," that is, they are not married to the mother and have not established paternity. The issues discussed earlier regarding identifying, locating, notifying, and engaging fathers are relevant to incarcerated fathers. While the mother may finally reveal the father's identity, she may or may not know if he is incarcerated. Best practice in cases involving incarcerated fathers includes:

- Ensure the caseworker confirms the father's incarceration status. With a name, a birth date, and possibly other information, the caseworker should be able to locate an incarcerated father quickly.
- Insist that the caseworker contact the alleged father, inform him of the legal proceedings, and determine his desires regarding the child welfare proceedings. The fact that he is in jail should not stop the inquiry.[68]
- Bring the incarcerated father to court, appoint counsel, have paternity established, and proceed with the case.[69]
- Offer services to incarcerated fathers who show interest in reunifying with their children, including visitation, to improve their parenting abilities.[70] Even if services are unavailable in prison (counseling, parenting classes, etc.), insist that the caseworker assist the father and examine the caseworker's conduct as part of the reasonable efforts requirement.[71]
- Be creative in efforts to involve incarcerated fathers. In one New Hampshire judicial district the court has approved a computer hook-up in the jail so that incarcerated fathers can communicate with their children.[72]

(See Chapter 8, *Representing Incarcerated Nonresident Fathers*, for more guidance.)

Conclusion

Our court traditions and practices must change to embrace fathers, and judges must take the lead. Recent developments in law and practice are encouraging. Increasingly legislatures are passing laws that grant fathers the same rights as mothers once paternity is established. Additionally, the extended family is now a placement of choice if children must be removed from their parents.

It is up to the court to ensure fathers receive their legal rights, lawyers speak forcefully for them, and caseworkers fulfill their roles in identifying, locating, notifying, and working with fathers. The potential benefits are that the father will become engaged in the court process and with his child, and the father and his family will be a resource to the child and to the decision makers in the court system. Additionally, allowing the child to remain with family brings emotional, social, and financial rewards for the child.

The author thanks Judge William Jones (ret.), David Meyers, and Bruce Boyer for their assistance in writing this chapter and Alan Hertzberg and Sean Marsh for their research assistance. The author also thanks all of the judicial officers who gave their thoughts about the issues raised in the chapter.

Endnotes

1. "Child welfare proceedings" is used in this chapter to refer to legal proceedings brought on behalf of allegedly abused, neglected, or abandoned children. The infrequency of fathers' involvement has been noted in Malm, K., J. Murray and R. Geen. *What about the Dads? Child Welfare Agencies' Efforts to Identify, Locate and Involve Nonresident Fathers.* Washington, D.C.: U.S. Department of Health and Human Services, Office of the Assistant Secretary of Planning and Evaluation, 2006, vii–xiii.

2. Supporting documentation on file with the author.

3. National Child Welfare Resource Center for Family-Centered Practice. "Father Involvement in Child Welfare: Estrangement and Reconciliation." *Best Practice/Next Practice,* Summer 2002, 1-2.

4. U.S. Commission on Child and Family Welfare. *Parenting Our Children: In the Best Interest of the Nation, A Report to the President and Congress,* 1996, 1; Green, A. "Policy and Practice Reform to Engage Non-Resident Fathers in Child Welfare Proceedings (Part 1)." *Child CourtWorks* 10(5), Aug. 2008; Popenoe, D. "Life Without Father." In *Lost Fathers,* edited by C. Daniels. New York: St. Martin's Griffin, 1998, 33-49; McClanahan, S. "Growing Up Without Father." In *Lost Fathers,* edited by C. Daniels. New York: St. Martin's Griffin, 1998, 87-108.

5. "Putative fathers must be located and brought into court process as quickly as possible." *Adoption and Permanency Guidelines: Improving Court Practice in Child Abuse and Neglect Cases.* Reno, NV: National Council of Juvenile and Family Court Judges (NCJFCJ), 2000, 10.

6. "Timely resolution of paternity issues is both in the best interests of the child and essential to avoiding delays at subsequent points in the court process." NCJFCJ, *Adoption Guidelines,* 2000, 10.

7. *E.g.,* State ex rel. DHS v. Rardin, 134 P.3d 940 (Or. 2006); In re Shaiesha O., 887 A.2d 415 (Conn. App. Ct. 2006); In re Deztiny C., 723 N.W.2d 652 (Neb. Ct. App. 2006); In re Dylan Z., 697 N.W.2d 707 (Neb. Ct. App. 2005).

8. Parke, M. "Are Married Parents Really Better for Children? What Research Says about the Effects of Family Structure on Child Well-Being." Washington, D.C.: Center for Law and Social Policy, 2003; McLanahan, S. and G. Sandefur. *Growing Up with a Single Parent: What Hurts, What Helps.* Cambridge, MA: Harvard Univ. Press, 1994.

9. Edwards, L. and I. Sagatun-Edwards. "The Transition to Group Decision Making in Child Protection Cases: Obtaining Better Results for Children and Families." *Juvenile and Family Court Journal* 58(1), Winter 2007, 8-9; Beck, K. et al. "Finding Family Connections for Foster Youth." *ABA Child Law Practice* 27(8), October 2008, 113-125.

10. Children living without fathers are five times more likely to be poor. U.S. Census Bureau. "Children's Living Arrangements and Characteristics: March 2002." *Current Population Reports*, Pub. No. 20-547, June 2003.

11. Some states require the paternity enquiry at the initial hearing. *See* Cal. Welf. & Inst. Code § 316.2(a) and Cal. Rule of Court 1413(b). This is a best practice since it focuses upon a critical issue at the earliest court hearing. *See also* Edwards, L. "Achieving Timely Permanency in Child Protection Courts: The Importance of Frontloading the Court Process." *Juvenile and Family Court Journal* 58(2), Spring 2007.

12. This follow-up by the social worker is important. If the divorce was never finalized (and often it has not been), this man is the father of the child since he and she were married at the time of the conception and birth. However, biologically someone else is the father of the child. If the husband can be found, he is entitled to notice. Usually, he tells the social worker or comes to court and states he is not the father and does not want any involvement in the case.

13. The issue of payment for paternity testing has been raised in several states. It is in the best interests of the child, the family, and the court process that paternity be established as soon as possible. The state has an interest in this determination and should be responsible for the cost of the testing. Since the state also has an interest in identifying fathers for child support purposes, caseworkers should be ready to work in tandem with child support authorities to complete paternity testing. Putting the burden on the father to arrange for blood or DNA testing or requiring him to file a paternity action is unduly burdensome and unrealistic, particularly if he is indigent, and it is also time consuming. Additionally, it is in the best interests of the child to have paternity established as soon as possible. Some courts have located a genetic testing site within the courthouse. This convenience can save days and weeks in the paternity-determination process. Cook County (Chicago) is a model for this practice.

14. In some courts the question of paternity can and is determined immediately. If the parties are living together and each claims that the person claiming to be father is indeed the father, the court could place both parties under oath, examine them about their relationship, advise the father of his right to have a formal court hearing on the issue of paternity, advise the father of the rights and responsibilities relating to a paternity determination, and make a finding of paternity. If there is any question about the issue, the DNA or other testing is necessary. If the father has any questions about the legal issues, a lawyer should be appointed before the paternity examination and finding.

15. *See generally* Iowa Code § 232.91(1); S.D. Codified Laws § 25-6-1.1; Va. Code Ann. § 16.1-277.01 B4; Fla. Stat. Ann. § 63.062; Idaho Code Ann. § 16-1505 (2) et. seq.

16. Uniform Parentage Act, available at www.nccusl.org.

17. D.C. Code § 16-2304.

18. In Nevada, indigent parents do not have a legal right to representation, so only have representation in a few circumstances where the judge orders it. This is also true in Indiana. In Minnesota, as of the date of this writing, the Office of the Public Defender has stopped representing parents so there are no state-funded lawyers for indigent parents in the child welfare system.

19. The National Center for Health Statistics reports that 36.9% of all births in the United States in 2005 were to unmarried mothers, another all-time high. Available at www.cdc.gov/nchs/fastats/birth/htm.

20. *See, e.g.*, Pickett v. Brown, 462 U.S. 1, 7 (1983)("…imposing disabilities on the illegitimate child is contrary to the basic concept of our system that legal burdens should bear some relationship to individual responsibility or wrongdoing…the Equal Protection Clause does enable us to strike down discriminatory laws relating to status of birth"); Gomez v Perez, 409 U.S. 535, 538 (1973)("a State may not invidiously discriminate against illegitimate children by denying them substantial benefits accorded children generally.").

21. For a discussion of these issues, cases and statutes, *see* Harris, L. "Involving Nonresident Fathers in Dependency Cases: New Efforts, New Problems, New Solutions." *Journal of Law and Family Studies* 9(2), 2007, 301-307. *Also see* Chapter 1 in this book.

22. The Adoption Assistance and Child Welfare Act of 1980, P.L. 96-272, 42 U.S.C. § 670 et. seq.

23. Items 13, 18 and 20, Child and Family Services Review. The CFSR results from almost every state have been disappointing in all of these measures.

24. "The court must ensure that the efforts of the child welfare agency are thorough and diligent in locating and involving all legal and putative fathers." NCJFCJ, *Adoption Guidelines*, 2000, 10.

25. This chapter uses "shelter care hearing" to refer to the first hearing in a child welfare case.

26. In some states, failure to conduct a thorough investigation can result in reversal of a termination of parental rights decision. *See* In re S.P., 672 N.W.2d 842, 848 (Iowa 2003) ("For example, the investigator did not talk to the children or their caretaker, Scott, or to the children's mother.").

27. "Family finding" emphasizes the importance of family members as a solution to the problems facing abused and neglected children. *See* Edwards, "Achieving Timely Permanency," 2007, 8; Beck et al., October 2008.

28. On the use of the "no reasonable efforts" finding, *see* Edwards, L. "Improving Implementation of the Adoption and Child Welfare Act of 1980." *Juvenile and Family Court Journal* 45(3), 1994, 19-23; Edwards, L. "Reasonable Efforts: A Judicial Perspective." *The Judge's Page*, July 2008, available at www.Nationalcasa.org.

29. State v. Corrigan, 600 S.W.2d. 87 (Mo. Ct. App. 1980); Minn. Stat. Ann. § 259.49, subd. 1; Iowa Code § 232.91(1). Iowa's restrictive statute has not prevented Iowa judges from taking a more proactive attitude towards the identification, notice, and engagement of nonresident fathers in child welfare cases, however.

30. 705 Ill. Comp. Stat. 405 1-3(11), 405 1-5(1), 405 1-5(1.5), 405 2-10(3); Nolan, L. "Preventing Fatherlessness through Adoption While Protecting the Parental Rights of Unwed Fathers: How Effective Are Paternity Registries?" *Whittier Journal of Child and Family Advocacy* 4, Spring 2005, 289-322 (noting that fathers do not know about the registry and that registries are ineffective in interstate adoptions).

31. 705 Ill. Comp. Stat. 405 2-10(4).

32. 705 Ill. Comp. Stat. 405 2-15, 2-16.

33. The social worker must make the court aware of facts that might lead it to conclude that visits would harm the child.

34. E-mail correspondence from Commissioner Marilyn Kading Martinez, June 12, 2008 ("... what is very very important is to treat the man with dignity and respect. The goal is for him to feel that he is being treated fairly and that he can be a part of his child's life and we will take him seriously.") Copy available from the author.

35. In 1981, in Lassiter v. Department of Social Services, 452 U.S. 18, the United States Supreme Court ruled that due process does not always require the appointment of counsel in termination of parental rights cases. Since child welfare proceedings are less intrusive than termination of parental rights, it is logical to conclude there is no constitutional right to counsel in child welfare proceedings.

36. National Council of Juvenile and Family Court Judges. *Child Abuse and Neglect: Representation as a Critical Component of Effective Practice,* March 1998. States not requiring appointment of counsel for indigent parents include DE, ID, KY, IN, MN and MS. However, a statute requiring appointment of counsel for indigent parents does not always mean the trial court will implement the statute. Nevada, for example, has been sued for failing to appoint counsel for indigent parents (and for children as well).

37. Ibid.

38. Garcia, S. and R. Batey. "Parents, Children, and the Courts: The Roles of Counsel for the Parent in Child Dependency Proceedings." *Georgia Law Review* 22, 1988, 1079, 1093-94.

39. The court's role in overseeing the provision of legal services to indigent parents is important. One state has written a Standard of Judicial Administration that addresses this issue. *See* California Standard of Judicial Administration 5.40(c) (West, 2008).

40. Ibid.

41. *See* San Francisco Superior Court, *Local Rules of Court,* Rule 12.6–12.18, describing an elaborate system for identifying qualified parent lawyers.

42. Judge Carolyn Kirkwood, presiding judge, Orange County (CA) Juvenile Court. Research shows that connections with families can refocus a parent's attitude towards life, even a life of crime. Desistance from crime is one of the byproducts. *See* Farrall, S. *Rethinking What Works With Offenders.* Portland: Willan Publishing, 2002, 8, 146, 152, 159.

43. Ibid.

44. *See* In re Baby Boy V., 45 Cal. Rptr. 3d 198 (Ct. App. 2006) involving trial court's failure to notify and engage father in child welfare proceedings, resulting in reversal of termination of parental rights order and remand for new trial.

45. Farrall, S. and A. Calverley. *Understanding Desistance from Crime.* New York: Open University Press, 2006, 72; Farrall, *Rethinking What Works,* 2002.

46. *See, e.g.,* Cal. Welf. & Inst. Code § 361.3(a) (West, 2008) which states, in part, "In any case in which a child is removed from the physical custody of his or her parents pursuant to Section 361, preferential consideration shall be given to a request by a relative of the child for placement of the child with the relative." Recent federal legislation places great emphasis on the identification and engagement of relatives. *See* Fostering Connections to Success and Increasing Adoptions Act of 2008, P.L. 110-351.

47. Edwards and Sagatun-Edwards, 2007, 8-9.

48. The AFCARs data shows approximately 24% of children in out-of-home care reside with relatives.

49. Such protocols are standard practice in some jurisdictions. *See* Cal. Rule of Court 5.215. For discussion of best practices regarding mediation when domestic violence issues are present, *see* Edwards, "Achieving Timely Permanency," 2007, 12-13.

50. *See* Edwards, L. "Comments on the Miller Commission Report: A California Perspective." *Pace Law Review* 27(4), Summer 2007, 635-639.

51. The California legislature has acknowledged the importance of nonadversarial resolution of family matters. *See* Cal. Welf. & Inst. Code § 350, Cal. Fam. Code § 3170(a), and the California Blue Ribbon Commission on Foster Care, Recommendation 2E, www.courtinfo.ca.gov/jc/tlists/bluerib.htm.

52. Other common names for such processes are family group decision making, family group conferencing, team decision making, family team meetings, and court-based mediation. *See* Edwards and Sagatun-Edwards, "Group Decision Making," 2007; For a description of family team meetings, *see* Edwards, "Achieving Timely Permanency," 2007, 13-14; MacRae, A. and H. Zehr. *The Little Book of Family Group Conferences: New Zealand Style*. Intercourse, PA: The Little Books of Justice & Peacebuilding, Good Books, 2004; *Family Group Conferencing*, edited by Burford, G. and J. Hudson. Piscataway, NJ: Aldine Transaction, 2005.

53. E-mail correspondence from Donna Hand, deputy director to Judge Susan Huguenor, presiding judge of the San Diego County Juvenile Court, July 31, 2008. Copy available from the author.

54. *See* Edwards, L. "Mediation in Child Protection Cases." *Journal of the Center for Families, Children & the Courts* 5, 2004, 57-69; Trosch, L. et. al. "Child Abuse, Neglect, and Dependency Mediation Pilot Project." *Juvenile and Family Court Journal* 53(4), Fall 2002, 57-67; and the citations in Edwards, "Achieving Timely Permanency," 2007, 12-13. If you are interested in starting a child welfare mediation program, contact the author for a free DVD. E-mail: leonard.edwards@jud.ca.gov.

55. Edwards, L., et al. "Mediation in Juvenile Dependency Court: Multiple Perspectives." *Juvenile and Family Court Journal* 53(4), Fall 2002.

56. Ibid.

57. Any visiting relatives must not pose a threat of harm to the child.

58. Beyer, M. "Visit Coaching: Building on Family Strengths to Meet Children's Needs." *Juvenile and Family Court Journal* 59(1), Winter 2008, 47-60.

59. E-mail from Marty Beyer, October 18, 2008. Copy available from the author.

60. Edwards et al., "Mediation in Dependency Court," 2003, 10.

61. E-mail from Joe Spaeth, Marin County Public Defender, September 30, 2008. Mr. Spaeth's office represents parents in child welfare proceedings. Copy of e-mail available from the author.

62. For an outstanding example of such parenting programs, *see* www.celebratingfamilies.net/.

63. Effective programs for fathers in Colorado include B.A.M. (Be a Man) Fatherhood Program in the Greeley/Evans area (www.realdads.net); Got Fatherhood? Program in South Weld County (Longmont/Boulder) (www.gotfatherhood.com), and Colorado Dads—Be There for Your Kids, a state program (www.coloradodads.com). The Center on Fathering in Colorado Springs, CO also offers several programs for fathers, and is a model intervention/evaluation site for the Quality Improvement Center on Non-Resident Fathers and the Child Welfare System. For advice about maximizing the effectiveness of fathers' programs, *see* Rosenberg and Wilcox, Office on Child Abuse and Neglect. "The Importance of Fathers in the Healthy Development of Children" (CD-ROM). *User Manual Series*, 2006.

64. Brandon, E. "Dudley Morgan Speaks about Marin City Fatherhood Program." *The Center View* (a publication of the Marin City Community Services District), 10(20), Oct-Nov, 2008, 4.

65. For a discussion on how a "no reasonable efforts" finding can result in changes to services available in the community, *see* Edwards, L. "Improving Implementation of the Adoption and Child Welfare Act of 1980." *Juvenile and Family Court Journal* 45(3), 1994, 3; Appendix C, in *Resource Guidelines: Improving Court Practice in Child Abuse & Neglect Cases.* Reno, NV: National Council of Juvenile and Family Court Judges, 1995, 167-168; Edwards, L. "Reasonable Efforts: A Judicial Perspective," July 2008.

66. E-mail correspondence with Child Support Commissioner John Schroeder, June 4, 2008. Copy available from the author.

67. Committee on Law and Justice. *Parole, Desistance from Crime, and Community Integration.* Washington, D.C.: National Research Council, 2007.

68. Additionally, connecting with family can change the direction of a prisoner's life. *See* Farrall, *Rethinking What Works,* 2002.

69. Ibid.

70. California legislation permits the court to extend the reunification period for parents who are incarcerated, institutionalized, or in residential substance abuse treatment up to 24 months from the time the child was removed from the parent under specified circumstances. The statute requires the court to consider the parent's criminal history as well as the parent's ability to care for the child. AB 2070 (Ch. 842, Statutes of 2008). This is a clear legislative determination that the facts surrounding incarceration should be carefully considered before ending the parent-child relationship.

71. Lough, D. "Incarcerated Father Entitled to Reunification Services." *Journal of Juvenile Law* 21, 2000, 169-173; *See also* In re Robin V., 39 Cal. Rptr. 2d 743 (Ct. App. 1995).

72. E-mail correspondence from Judge Susan B. Carbon, Grafton County, NH, October 12, 2008. Copy available from the author.

CHAPTER SIX

Addressing Special Advocacy Issues

Andrew L. Cohen

CHECKLIST

Addressing Special Advocacy Issues

Substance abuse

➤ Be discerning about when and how much information you share with the court regarding your client's substance abuse issues.

➤ Urge your client to speak openly with you about his history of substance abuse problems so you can advance his goals and advocate for proper treatment.

➤ Be mindful of statutory timelines and promptly identify appropriate treatment and services.

➤ Even if the evidence of abuse is unassailable, challenge the agency's attempts to tie the father's substance abuse to his parental fitness.

Mental health concerns

➤ Ask your client to sign releases to allow you to speak with his mental health care providers. Remind him of attorney-client privileges.

➤ Ensure greater confidentiality by seeking services from a local mental health clinic rather than through the court clinic.

➤ Only request a guardian ad litem (GAL) for your father client in extraordinary circumstances when his capacity to make significant decisions is truly diminished. Be sure to have the court clearly define the GAL's role so that it does not supplant or undermine the father's stated wishes or goals for the case.

Domestic violence allegations

➤ Investigate allegations of domestic violence by interviewing law enforcement, agency workers, and the mother (if counsel will allow) and reviewing documentary evidence carefully. Determine the source of the allegations and whether they are true.

- Explain to your client whether domestic violence evaluations are confidential. Help him weigh the benefits of cooperating with case plan goals.
- If your client decides to challenge the agency's allegations, provide the agency and court exculpatory evidence and favorable information as soon as possible.

Immigration concerns

- Consult an immigration lawyer or specialist for assistance.
- Counsel your client on whether going to court may negatively impact his situation if there is an outstanding immigration detainer.

Download this and other checklists at **www.fatherhoodqic.org/checklists**

Your client wants custody of his daughter. The child welfare agency removed her from her mother and is unwilling to place her with your client. The agency alleges that he is an alcoholic and has physically abused the mother. As you investigate the case, you determine the allegations have merit. Further, your client discloses to you that he is bipolar and that he rarely takes his medication. In your office, he thanks you for all the work you are going to do for him, and tells you that his family is in your hands. How do you proceed?

As the lawyer for the nonresident father, you must help him determine the right course of action, considering his wishes, strengths, and limitations. You will need to work with the agency to negotiate an appropriate case plan. You may also need to independently determine the services your client needs. If a cooperative resolution of the case is not possible, you must be prepared with evidence to rebut the agency's allegations against your client.

The following discussion will help you address some common problems nonresident fathers face in the child welfare system. This chapter is not exhaustive, but it gives you some ideas for how best to accomplish your clients' goals.

Substance Abuse

Many child welfare cases involve parental drug or alcohol use, abuse, or addiction.[1] Substance abuse is not just a terrible problem for parents to address; allegations of substance abuse are very difficult for lawyers to rebut.

Communication and investigation

To start, explain to the father the agency's allegations of substance abuse and the evidence the agency has (or claims to have) to support those allegations. He may deny that he uses or abuses alcohol or illegal drugs. He may confirm the substance use but deny that it impairs his parenting. Or he may agree that the allegations are true and he needs treatment.

Do not pursue a strategic direction yet; you need more information about your client and his needs. Urge him to speak openly to you about his history of substance use and abuse. Make sure he is aware of the rules of attorney-client confidentiality, and that you will not disclose to the agency or law enforcement any substance use he admits to you.[2] You cannot understand your client's history and needs, or advocate for proper treatment to advance his goals, if you have inadequate information. If you need assistance to determine his needs, ask the court for funds for an expert to perform a confidential substance abuse evaluation. (File your request *ex parte*, if your rules allow, to avoid disclosing information to the agency and other parties. Do not, at this stage, ask the court to

When a Father Relapses

Relapse is Normal

Substance abusing and addicted clients often relapse after entering treatment. While it can happen at any time during recovery,[1] relapse often occurs shortly before trial. Trial is stressful for parents, and stressful events trigger relapses.[2] Relapse is not the same as failure of treatment; it is normative.[3] What matters is your client's commitment upon returning to treatment.

Trial=Stress=Relapse

Sometimes relapse on the eve of trial signifies the father's own doubts about his ability to parent. The father may struggle with low self-esteem and lack confidence. It is not surprising that some fathers believe that they cannot handle the responsibility of caring for a child. You should work closely with the client to determine how he feels about trial and the possibility of reunification. Work closely with his treatment providers to ensure they are aware of trial dates in order to monitor your client's stress.

Sources:
1. Breshears, Elizabeth M., Shaila Yeh and Nancy K. Young. *Understanding Substance Abuse and Facilitating Recovery: A Guide for Child Welfare Workers.* Washington, D.C.: U.S. Department of Health and Human Services, 2005, 18 [Pub. No. (SMA) 05-3981].
2. *Stress and Substance Abuse: A Special Report.* Bethesda, MD: National Institute on Drug Abuse, available at www.drugabuse.gov/stressanddrugabuse.html (last accessed 04/06/09), and studies cited therein.
3. Breshears et al., 2005, 18.

appoint a substance abuse evaluator or refer the father to the court clinic. Such evaluations are generally shared with the agency, other counsel and the court, and you do not yet know if the client is best served by sharing or withholding the information.) If your evaluation suggests that the father does *not* have a problem, consider sharing it with the agency (with your client's consent) to keep unnecessary services off his case plan. If the evaluation shows that he needs treatment, do not share it (although it may later prove useful in negotiating a case plan); rather, use it to urge your client to participate in appropriate services. Explain to him that treatment is vital if he wants custody of his child. The agency and the courts often support reunification efforts for fathers who seek, and faithfully participate in, treatment.

Regular communication with the substance abusing or addicted father may be difficult. He may not have steady housing or telephone service. He may not answer the door or the phone while using drugs. He may pass in and out of detox-ification programs and hospitals. Generally, such facilities will not confirm his presence absent a release. You must leave messages for him in the hope he is there and will return the call. Keep handy a list of addresses and phone numbers of local detoxification centers, shelters, and hospitals.

Services

There are many services for substance addicted and abusing parents.[3] Many state health and human services or public health departments list counseling programs, day-treatment programs and residential programs on their Web sites.[4]

Treatment can be a long-term commitment. Fathers with chronic substance abuse problems may need one to two years to stabilize in recovery.[5] Neither the Adoption and Safe Families Act (ASFA) nor most state child welfare statutes ac-commodate such a schedule. Permanency hearings must take place within 12 months of the initial custody order to the agency.[6] If the father is not actively in-volved in treatment, the court might approve a goal of adoption and determine that the agency need no longer provide reunification services. Accordingly, there is little leeway for relapses or the father's inability to complete one program and need to start afresh elsewhere. (See *When a Father Relapses* box.) While some judges may delay a trial to accommodate your client's "graduation" from a pro-gram, others will not. You must push, both in and out of court, for the agency to provide necessary services and referrals.

Carefully negotiate the case plan with the agency. Your father client must enter treatment quickly, and the program must match his needs. Consider re-taining an expert (or asking the expert you used for any initial evaluation) to rec-ommend appropriate treatment programs for the client. Do not delay. An expert hired on the eve of trial who testifies that the father needs certain treatments that the agency failed to provide is unlikely to sway a court to return a child or delay termination.

Waitlists for treatment programs, especially inpatient programs, can be long. ASFA deadlines will not wait. Discuss with your client the possibility of negoti-ating with the agency for placement of the child with a relative. Such placements allow the agency to delay filing termination petitions.[7] This may buy your client enough time to get into, or finish, the right program.

Because treatment can last so long and ASFA timelines are so short, your fa-ther client may be mid-treatment at the time of trial. If so, request a continuance until the end of his treatment. Courts are more likely to grant such requests if they are for a short period. If the court refuses to continue the start of trial, request that it begin trial on schedule but continue subsequent days until the father has finished the program. Alternatively, ask the court to stay the close of evidence (or agree to reopen the evidence) to allow the father and program staff to testify after he finishes the program.

Challenging agency allegations

Your client may deny that he has a substance abuse problem, refuse services, or fail in treatment. You have no choice, then, but to attempt to refute, or at least undermine, the agency's proof that the substance abuse renders him unfit. Determine and investigate the sources of the agency's information. Prepare to challenge the evidence in court by getting answers to these questions:

- **Does the agency have witnesses to your client's drug use?**
  Contact the witnesses (as permitted by ethical or other rules). If they, themselves, are drug-involved, determine if they can be located, are reliable and/or unbiased, and will come to court to testify even if subpoenaed. Determine their likely testimony; depose them if your court rules allow. Ask your client if other witnesses might contradict the sources or present the evidence in a better light. The agency may try to enter witness statements in evidence through police reports or agency records. If so, move to exclude the statements as hearsay if they do not satisfy any exceptions.

- **Does your client have one or more drug-related convictions?**
  Know the rules governing the admission of convictions and criminal history reports. Object if the agency attempts to introduce the records improperly. Move to strike portions of the criminal history report that are not probative of any offense, such as dismissals, continuances without a finding, and not-guilty verdicts. Object to the admission of older convictions on staleness grounds.

- **Does the agency have drug screens that show positive results for illegal drugs?** Learn about the testing underlying the screen results. Courts have excluded certain types of screens as unreliable.[8] Determine whether the agency will try to introduce them under the "business records," "medical records," or other hearsay exception. Object if the proper certifications or other foundational requirements are missing. Similarly, drug screens may be privileged under state or federal drug treatment statutes.[9] Know and assert such privileges.

Even if the evidence of the father's substance use is unassailable, that alone is generally not enough for the agency to prove unfitness. The agency must still show a connection between his substance use and poor parenting or risk of harm to the child.[10] Many judges assume such a connection exists, which places the burden on you to disprove it. To do so, make the following inquiries:

- During the time the father was using drugs, was he parenting the subject child (or other children)? If so, was he providing her with adequate food, supervision, medical care, and attention to other daily needs?
- Did he get her to school regularly, on time, and dressed appropriately?
- If he was visiting the child during a time he was using, was he appropriate, attentive, and affectionate during visits?
- During this period, was he able to hold a job, maintain housing, and refrain from illegal activities—that is, could he have maintained a stable environment for the child?

The answers to these questions dictate the evidence you must offer at trial to show the father can parent effectively regardless of his substance use.

In most cases, however, the agency will be able to show a connection between your client's substance use and risk of harm to the child. Then, if he has not participated successfully in treatment, the outcome of trial is clear. Explain to your client that he is unlikely to get custody. Further, unless the mother secures a return of custody and the case is dismissed, the most likely result of trial will be termination of his parental rights. Do some "concurrent planning" with him. Work together to locate his relatives or friends who may serve as guardianship or adoptive resources. Explore with him the possibility of an open adoption agreement to permit him some future contact with the child.

Mental Health Issues

The agency does not usually allege that a child is at risk simply because a father has a mental illness. Rather, the agency usually alleges some behavior that suggests an untreated mental illness; or, if the social worker is already familiar with the father and his mental health issues, the allegations may focus on his failure to seek or stay in treatment or his failure to regularly take his medication.

Communication and investigation

Discuss the agency's allegations with the father. He may be very uncomfortable discussing his mental health history with a stranger. You may need to meet with him several times to earn his trust. Make sure he understands the confidential nature of your conversations.

Learn about his current mental health providers and medications, if he has

■ Addressing Unfounded Allegations

The allegations raised by the child welfare agency—or another party—against the father may be unfounded or greatly exaggerated. In such circumstances, your client may be very angry that "trumped up" charges have, at least temporarily, deprived him of his child. Make sure he remains calm. Any demonstration of hostility—especially if the false allegations concern domestic violence—will make it difficult to negotiate an appropriate case plan with the agency and harm his chances in court.

Act Quickly

As a result of the false allegations, the agency may insist on inappropriate services. Or it may unnecessarily require that visits be supervised or reduced. It is therefore crucial that you aggressively challenge false allegations at the earliest opportunity. Send the social worker letters in support of your client and any other favorable documentation. Thoroughly prepare your client to address the allegations at any meeting at the agency. Make sure he can do so calmly; arrange to speak on his behalf if he cannot. Ask the worker or supervisor if you can bring any character or fact witnesses to the meeting.

Prepare for Court

You must be even more prepared to address any false allegations in court. Have your witnesses and documentary evidence ready for the initial post-removal hearing. Prepare your client to testify and be cross-examined. If the allegations arise later in the proceeding, bring the issue to the court's attention promptly. The longer the allegations remain unchallenged, the harder it will be to convince the court of their falseness.

Plan for Success

If you successfully rebut the allegations, you may be able to keep unnecessary services off your client's case plan. You may even be able to convince the court to grant the father custody of his child. Your aggressive defense of your client, both in and out of court, will assure him that you are his "champion" and that he will be "heard" by both the agency and the court.

Plan for a Loss

Make sure your client understands that he may not be vindicated. You may not be able to convince the agency to change the case plan; you may not win in court. If the mother tells the social worker or testifies that your client uses drugs or has been physically abusive, you may not, despite your best efforts to cross-examine or discredit her, be able to convince the agency or the court otherwise. If your client loses, the best way to preserve the lawyer-client relationship—and your client's chances to gain custody in the future—is to empathize with his disappointment and anger, but also to plan with him how to work cooperatively with the agency so that he can convince the agency and the court of his parental fitness later in the proceeding.

any. Have him sign releases so you can speak freely with any providers. If he is on any medications, learn what they are and what they are for. Ask his providers about his mental health history, diagnosis and prognosis, his attendance and commitment to treatment, and their assessment of his functioning on and off medication. Learn their opinions about his ability to parent.

If your client did not have providers before the filing of the child welfare case, consider seeking court funds for an expert to evaluate him and recommend appropriate treatment.

Services

The agency tends to put an evaluation and counseling on the case plan of every parent alleged to have mental health issues. This may be all your client needs. Do not allow the evaluation to be done by anyone who will share it with the agency and the court, such as the court clinic. Rather, have your client request the evaluation from a local mental health service. This ensures greater confidentiality. Have him sign releases so that you can speak freely to the providers, and remind them not to speak to the agency without speaking to you first. Or retain an expert to recommend services. Share the results of any evaluation only if they are favorable (and your client consents).

Your client may need more extensive services. He may need parenting classes specifically geared toward parents with similar needs and abilities. He may need day treatment or residential treatment that permits parents and children to stay together. Such programs may not exist in your area. If they do exist, they may have long waitlists or be far from the client's home. Negotiate with the agency to have all appropriate services on the case plan. Share your expert's recommendations, if strategically appropriate. ASFA requires that the agency provide parents with "reasonable efforts" to reunify the family if the child has been removed.[11] To be "reasonable," such efforts may need to include extensive referrals and coordination of service providers.[12] Remind the agency of this ongoing obligation, and bring the matter to the court's attention if the agency is not providing the necessary referrals and services.

Competence to direct litigation

If your client has serious mental health issues, he may not be capable of making decisions about the litigation.[13] This depends on many factors, including his "ability to articulate reasoning leading to a decision; variability of state of mind and ability to appreciate consequences of a decision; the substantive fairness of a decision; and the consistency of a decision with the known long-term commitments and values of the client."[14] Just because you disagree with the father does not mean he is "incompetent" or has diminished capacity. Clients are entitled to disagree with you; indeed, they are entitled to make *poor* decisions.

Rule 1.14(a) of the ABA Model Rules of Professional Conduct provides that, when a client's capacity to make adequately considered decisions is diminished because of mental impairment, "the lawyer shall, as far as reasonably possible, maintain a normal client-lawyer relationship with the client."[15] A "normal" relationship means that you owe the client, among other things, the duties of loyalty, confidentiality and diligence.[16] You must keep in regular contact with the father and inform him of case developments.

Your client may be competent to advise you and participate in some decisions but not others.[17] For example, he may tell you that he wants his sister to care for his child, although he does not understand the distinction between foster care, guardianship, and adoption. You should be guided by his wishes. Rule 1.14 allows you to decide how best to fulfill those wishes and protect his interests. It also allows you to seek guidance from others in making various decisions.[18]

The Model Rules allow you to ask the court to appoint a guardian ad litem (GAL) if your client has diminished capacity and is at risk of substantial harm.[19] Arguably, such risk exists whenever a client's child may be lost to the agency. But requesting, or acquiescing to another party's request for, a GAL has drawbacks. First, admitting the father is unable to make reasoned decisions all but confirms that he is unfit to care for his child. Second, if the GAL is appointed to "replace" the father as decision maker (an appointment known as a "next friend" in many jurisdictions), the appointment greatly disempowers the client.

Generally, you should request a GAL for the father only in extraordinary circumstances, and should contest a motion for appointment filed by another party. If a GAL is appointed, ensure that the court clearly defines the GAL's role.

Challenging agency allegations

Your client may deny that he has mental health issues and refuse to participate in treatment. (See *Addressing Unfounded Allegations* box.) Or he may participate but still fail to improve his functioning or ability to parent. You must then attempt to rebut the agency's allegation that your client has a mental health issue. If his mental health issues are beyond dispute, you must show that his illness does not present a risk of harm to his child.[20] Many parents with mental health issues can adequately care for their children without professional assistance or medication.

As noted earlier, consider retaining an expert to evaluate your client. The expert may be able to offer an opinion about your client's level of functioning or challenge prior diagnoses. The expert may be able to state that the client did not receive proper services from the agency, and that such services were available.[21]

If the father has been engaging in services, talk to his providers about his commitment to, and progress in, treatment. If their assessment is favorable, prepare them to testify and subpoena them if necessary.

Clients with serious mental health issues may have been hospitalized. The agency will often bring in such treatment records. Because these records represent your client at his worst, try to keep them out of evidence. Assert all applicable privileges. If the agency is seeking to admit the records under a hospital or medical records hearsay exception, ensure the agency has followed all statutory and common law rules for certifying and authenticating the records. Depending on the jurisdiction, not all hearsay and opinion in the records may be admissible. Therefore, review them promptly so you can move to exclude inadmissible portions before trial. Timely review will also allow you to discuss the records with your expert and, if necessary, subpoena hospital staff for cross-examination. If the court must review the records *in camera*, ensure it follows the prescribed procedures and object if it does not.

Domestic Violence

Communication and investigation

Domestic violence plays a significant role in child welfare cases.[22] Representing the alleged (or actual) perpetrator of domestic violence presents many challenges for the child welfare lawyer. The batterer may be dangerous to his partner, to other people and even to you. (See *When Your Client is Dangerous* box.) He may be facing criminal charges arising from the abusive acts. (See *Handling Concurrent Criminal Charges* box.)

If the batterer wants custody of his children, advocate zealously for this goal. But also seek to further his interests by helping prevent future violence.[23] Batterers who accept treatment and refrain from violent conduct are far more likely to gain (and keep) custody of their children.

Obtaining a factual history of the case and any past violence may be difficult. Most batterers present as rational, law-abiding, persuasive, and even charming.[24] They may claim that the partner is violent, suggesting that any physical confrontations were mutually aggressive or the batterer was defending himself.[25] Batterers also frequently minimize their abusive behavior. This may lead you to downplay or disbelieve the allegations of abuse. Indeed, many batterers do not understand that their behaviors are abusive; some do not understand that occasional or sporadic violence is also abuse. Early on, inform the father about the types of behaviors the courts consider abusive.

When Your Client is Dangerous

Threats to Partners

You may overhear the father threaten his partner or another person. He may communicate this threat to you directly. Consult your local ethics rules and opinions to determine how to proceed. Keep in mind that, in most jurisdictions, you can only breach a client confidence in limited circumstances. Many states' ethics rules provide that you may disclose a client communication to prevent commission of a criminal act that you reasonably believe is likely to result in death or substantial bodily injury to another.[1] Whether an overheard threat meets this high standard will depend on the circumstances.

Even the most violent batterers are unlikely to threaten the partner in court. But batterers often make nonverbal threats and gestures that the victim interprets (correctly) as threatening, but that others might assume are harmless.[2] Tell your client to refrain from making such gestures. If the judge catches on, he or she may throw your client out of court. The judge may even consider threatening gestures for evidentiary purposes.[3]

Threats to You

Fathers who abuse their partners or children may also treat you poorly. Keep detailed case notes in the event the batterer sues you or complains about you to the licensing authorities.[4] Take any threat of physical violence seriously. If you do not feel safe meeting with a violent client in his home or in your office alone, meet him in a public place. To preserve confidentiality, meet him at restaurants or coffee shops during off-peak hours or in private courthouse conference rooms. When meeting in isolated courthouse rooms, inform a court officer of the location of the meeting and ask the officer to knock on the door and check in with you periodically.

Sources:

1. *See* ABA Model Rules of Professional Conduct 1.6(b)(1); *cf.* Purcell v. District Atty. for Suffolk Dist., 424 Mass. 109, 110-16 (1997) (lawyer permitted to disclose client's communication of intent to burn building).

2. *See* Fischer, Karla et al. "The Culture of Battering and the Role of Mediation in Domestic Violence Cases." *Southern Methodist University Law Review* 46, 1993, 2117, 2120.

3. *See* O'Brien v. O'Brien, 347 Mass. 765, 766 (1964) (holding that court can consider demeanor of witness as evidence of custodial fitness).

4. *See* Quirion, Pauline. "Domestic Violence Issues." In 2 *Paternity and the Law of Parentage* § 12.6(b) (MCLE 2002), and sources cited therein.

Handling Concurrent Criminal Charges

The father may, as a result of the incidents giving rise to the child welfare case, be criminally charged or face potential criminal exposure. Or he may be arrested for an unrelated crime during the child welfare case. There are several stages in a child welfare proceeding that require your diligence.

Reports

CPS may (and, in some cases, must) notify and provide state prosecutors copies of reports of suspected abuse or neglect.[1] If you have been appointed by this time, ensure that the father understands the report will be turned over to law enforcement, and any statements he makes to CPS investigators may be admissible against him in the criminal action and the child welfare proceeding.

Interviews

In the child welfare case, CPS personnel, court-appointed investigators, and service providers may question the father about the charges. Other than certain mental health providers, most of these individuals have no confidential relationship with the father, and may be called by the prosecution to testify against him. Accordingly, you should:

➤ be present at all interviews of the father by CPS personnel, the court investigator, probation officers, and court clinicians or evaluators;

➤ carefully prepare him for such interviews;

➤ make sure he knows that any statements made to service providers, including during batterers' counseling, sex offender counseling, and parenting groups, may in certain circumstances be introduced in both the child welfare proceedings and the criminal proceedings;

➤ work out a plan for whether, or to whom, the client will speak about the incidents at issue;

➤ discuss all of the above with your client's criminal defense lawyer, and make sure he or she understands the procedures in the child welfare case and the consequences to your joint client of refusing to speak to providers and investigators.

Testimony

Whether or not the father testifies in the child welfare case is another concern. If he testifies, state law may give prosecutors access to the transcript. State law may also allow the prosecution to access records in the child welfare case. If the father asserts his Fifth Amendment right not to testify in the child welfare case, there may be other unpleasant consequences. Child welfare cases are civil matters, and the court may draw an adverse inference against the father if he fails or refuses to testify.[2] Such an inference may include deeming certain allegations by CPS admitted by the father.

This presents a Catch-22 for your client. If he wants custody of his child, he may need to testify. But if he testifies, he may be providing information to the prosecutor in the criminal case. Unfortunately, the best outcome for the father— a continuance of the child welfare case until the criminal matter is resolved—is rarely available. Delays, which are anathema to child welfare courts seeking speedy permanency for children, are common in criminal matters. The judge in the child welfare matter usually has broad discretion to grant or deny a continuance in this situation.[3] That discretion is rarely granted to accommodate parents with pending criminal matters.

Therefore, assume the child welfare trial will precede the criminal trial. Consult with criminal defense counsel and address the pros and cons of having the father testify. Ultimately, the choice of whether to testify rests with your client.[4]

Sources:

1. *See, e.g.,* G.L. Mass. c. 119, § 51B(k).

2. *See, e.g.,* Custody of Two Minors, 396 Mass. 610, 616 (1986); Care and Protection of Quinn, 54 Mass. App. Ct. 117, 121 (2002).

3. *See* Quinn, 54 Mass. App. Ct. at 120.

4. *See* Jones v. Barnes, 463 U.S. 745, 51 (1983); ABA Model Rule of Professional Conduct 1.2(a).

Do not assume the agency's allegations are groundless based purely on client interviews. Read the documentary evidence carefully, and determine the source of the allegations. A police response to an incident of violence may have triggered the filing of the child welfare case. If so, obtain copies of all reports. Interview the investigating or arresting officers if they are willing to speak to you. The mother may have told the agency social worker of the father's behavior. If so, ask her lawyer if you can speak to her about it (without the father present). If you cannot question her, request and review the social worker's notes (also known as dictation or "run sheets") to determine exactly what the mother has told the agency. Your client may have a long record of restraining order violations or domestic assault and battery convictions. If so, secure any required releases to run his criminal history report, and get an explanation from him about each offense.

Your client may concede that he has a problem and agree to treatment. Or you may be able to convince him that he is more likely to get custody of his child if he enters treatment. If the evidence against him is strong and he is reluctant to enter treatment, explain to him that he will likely lose custody, or even his parental rights, at trial.

Services

Agency case plans for alleged batterers usually include a domestic violence evaluation and, if the evaluation calls for it, batterer's treatment.[26] Explain to your client that such evaluations are rarely confidential. Any incriminating statements he makes are likely to end up in a report seen by the agency and the judge. You must work closely with the client to weigh the benefits of cooperating with the case plan against the potential drawbacks of disclosing violent conduct to the agency, the court, and potentially law enforcement personnel.

Treatment for batterers is conducted primarily in group sessions known as batterers' treatment or intervention programs.[27] Programs are long-term commitments. They may, depending on the state, require several sessions per week for up to a year. Programs often require the batterer to provide them with employer names, police reports, criminal records, and histories of substance abuse, mental illness, and abusive behaviors. Program staff generally communicates freely with the client's current partner and any prior victims. The batterer must admit to his violent acts. Explain to your client that such admissions may be entered in evidence in the child welfare case; they may also be admissible in a pending (or future) criminal case against him.

Become familiar with local batterer's treatment programs and their rules. The rules are strict, and the consequences to the client of being removed from a program may be severe. If he is participating to comply not just with the agency case plan but also with probation requirements, he may be surrendered and face jail time. Because the programs last so long, if he must start "fresh" at a second program, he is unlikely to complete it before trial in the child welfare case.

If the father is willing to participate in batterer's treatment, urge him to do so before the agency puts it on his case plan or before the court orders it. This will show his good faith and will give him a "jump" on long-term treatment.

Challenging agency allegations

You and your client may decide to challenge the agency's allegations of domestic violence. Your client may not have committed the acts alleged. Or the agency's evidence may be thin or stale. Provide the agency with exculpatory evidence and favorable information about the father as early in the case as possible. For example, if your client has a new partner with whom he's lived, violence-free, for many years, ask her to speak to the agency. Make sure the agency knows if his partner, friends, or relatives believe he is a loving, gentle caretaker to his or other children. If the agency agrees that your client does not pose a danger to his child, it may not put unnecessary services on his case plan.

If the agency remains unconvinced, and your client is unwilling to participate in services for batterers, you have no choice but to try to rebut or undermine the agency's proof. Object to admission of the father's criminal history report, or move to strike any portions of it that are not probative of unfitness (such as dismissals or not-guilty findings) or are stale. Prepare to cross-examine the sources of the allegations. If the agency intends to present the information through its social worker or reports, object to all hearsay statements that do not satisfy exceptions. Have your client identify any character or rebuttal witnesses, and subpoena them for trial.

If the agency is able to prove that your client is or has been violent, it will be difficult to argue that there is no nexus between his conduct and risk of harm to the child. In some states, courts presume that batterers should not have custody; in other states, courts cannot give the batterer custody absent specific findings that, despite the abuse, the child's best interests are served by such an order.[28] This is a difficult hurdle to overcome.[29] Most judges acknowledge that batterers present many dangers to children, even if they never direct their violence to the children themselves.[30]

Immigration Issues

Status

Many fathers in child welfare cases have immigration issues. Neither the agency nor the courts usually consider immigration status alone as determinative of parental unfitness. It is, however, a factor courts consider. Judges are loath to return children to parents who face detention and/or deportation.

Immigration law is highly specialized, and few child welfare lawyers practice it regularly. If your client is in the country illegally, consult an immigration lawyer or other immigration specialist for assistance.[31] In addition, attend trainings and read articles on immigration law.[32] Many agencies assist people with immigration problems. Either you or your client should consult the U.S. Citizenship and Immigration Services Web site, www.uscis.gov.

Immigration issues arise in several ways. Your client may have entered the country illegally, or he may have entered it legally with a "nonimmigrant visa"[33] but overstayed the visa. Foreign tourists and students generally are not allowed

Addressing Language Barriers

Your father client may speak little or no English. He may speak it clearly but not understand the nuances of your speech. For fathers who speak English but are not fluent, you can use several methods to aid communication.

Basic communication skills

Be patient and allow extra time for communication, and never overload him with information. Use simple language, such as, "Where do you live?" instead of "What is your place of residence?"[1] Speak slowly, but not loudly, when the father does not understand. Be wary of using hand signals or gestures, which may mean something else in his language or culture and may confuse him.

Interpreters

You may need an interpreter to help the father in and out of court.[2] Determine the language and dialect spoken by the father to ensure he receives the *right* interpreter. Many countries have more than one widely-spoken language, and words in the same language often differ in different countries.[3] For example, certain Spanish terms have different meanings to speakers from Puerto Rico and those from Mexico.[4] Also be careful to use interpreters who are familiar with child welfare court practice. You may need to familiarize the interpreter with the legal terms and procedures.[5]

Family members as interpreters

Circumstances may require that you use one of the father's family members or friends to interpret. Do not ask relatives who have an interest in the proceeding to interpret for you, unless your client supports that interest. Remember that the accuracy of the translation will depend on that person's comprehension and translation skills. An unskilled interpreter may summarize your wording, thereby leaving out crucial information. He or she may also attempt to "explain" some of your language, thereby conveying inaccurate and misleading information to the father. Further, in some circumstances, using an informal interpreter may waive attorney-client privilege and render the family member or friend an unwitting witness in the case. This is not to say that the use of informal interpreters is never appropriate; rather, it should be done only when absolutely necessary, when there is no time to obtain the services of a certified interpreter.

Translation services

For some simple communications—letters to set up meetings with the client or reminders about court dates—online translation services may be useful.

Use them with care, and make sure your client understands the translations generated by the site. A few to consider:

➤ **Freetranslation:** www.freetranslation.com

➤ **Promt-online:** http://translation2.paralink.com

➤ **Babel Fish:** http://babelfish.yahoo.com

Sources:

1. *See* Mahony, Dianne E. "Language and Communication Skills for Effective Cross-Cultural Communication." In *Ensuring Equal Justice: Addressing Cultural and Linguistic Differences in the Courts of Massachusetts*. Boston: Massachusetts Bar Association 1996, 17.

2. For more information on the role of and best practices for court interpreters, *see* National Center for State Courts. *Court Interpretation Resource Guide*, available at www.ncsconline.org/WC/CourTopics/ResourceGuide.asp?topic=CtInte.

3. *See* Reagan, Helen E. "Considerations in Litigating a Civil Case with Non-English Speaking Clients." *American Jurisprudence Trials* 65, 2004 1, §4.

4. Ibid.

5. For a discussion of the mechanics of court interpreting at trial and the proper use of an interpreter, *see* Grabau, Charles M. and Llewellyn J. Gibbons. "Protecting the Rights of Linguistic Minorities: Challenges to Court Interpretation." *Northeastern Law Review* 30, Winter 1996, 231.

to work, and doing so violates their visa status. Certain types of temporary non-immigrant visas allow the holder to work, but others do not. The fact that your client has a U.S. citizen child does not give him any legal status in the U.S. The child cannot petition for his "alien" father to live permanently in the U.S. until the child reaches age 21. Fathers with U.S. citizen children may be deported; either the child goes with the father or stays behind.

If your father client is an undocumented alien, he may be uncomfortable speaking to you about his circumstances. Encourage him to speak openly and honestly. Remind him about the rules of attorney-client confidentiality. (See *Addressing Language Barriers* and *Cultural Sensitivity and Fathers* boxes.)

Immigration consequences in child welfare

Your client may be wary of appearing in court, fearing the judge or probation officer will hold him for Immigration and Customs Enforcement ("ICE"). This fear is founded if your client has an outstanding immigration detainer; the court may then inform ICE that it is holding an undocumented alien. If your father client does not have an outstanding detainer, the court is unlikely to contact ICE.

Absent an outstanding immigration detainer, there is no federal requirement that judges or other court officials report information to ICE about the status of a suspected undocumented alien. But there is also nothing prohibiting such a

Cultural Sensitivity and Fathers

Fathers in child welfare cases come from every country and every ethnic, religious, and cultural group. Be sensitive to cultural differences when dealing with fathers from countries or ethnic groups that are unfamiliar to you. For resources on cultural sensitivity and competence, see:

➤ Cultural Competence, Child Welfare Information Gateway
www.childwelfare.gov/systemwide/cultural
Provides resources on cultural competence in the child welfare context.

➤ National Center for State Courts, Best Practices Institute: Racial Fairness
www.ncsconline.org/WC/Publications//BestPrac/BPRacFai.htm
Lists resources on combating racial bias in the courts.

➤ Izawa-Hayden, Althea. "Promoting Culturally Competent Legal Services for Latino Families." *ABA Child Law Practice* 24(2), April 2005, 17.

➤ Howze, Karen A. *Making Differences Work: Cultural Context in Abuse and Neglect Practice for Judges and Attorneys.* Washington, D.C.: ABA Center on Children and the Law, 1996.

report. Whether or not to report the father depends on local court rules and practices, and the discretion of court personnel, the agency, or other parties or counsel to the child welfare case. Upon receiving a report, immigration officials may issue a detainer for the alien to be held for up to 48 hours for ICE to determine whether to take custody of him.[34]

Your client's behavior—particularly regarding criminal activity—and his substance abuse and mental health status may have consequences in immigration proceedings.[35] Consult an immigration lawyer or specialist before advising your client in this regard.

Conclusion

Representing a nonresident father is particularly challenging when the agency alleges he is unfit. Your client may need services to address his substance abuse, mental health, domestic violence, or other problems. Becoming familiar with the relevant services in your area will help when negotiating an appropriate case plan with the agency. If your client refuses services or fails in treatment, challenge the agency's unfitness allegations in court. This entails thoroughly investigating the sources of the allegations and, once the matter is in court, making all necessary objections based on the rules of evidence and privilege. In some circumstances, an expert may help convince the court that the agency's allegations are unfounded or exaggerated and the father is capable of parenting his child. Most importantly, maintain regular communication with your client to clearly understand his wishes and needs as the case progresses.

Nonresident fathers may be—or may become—excellent custodial parents. Their opportunity to prove this to CPS and the court depends on your zealous and informed advocacy.

The author thanks Wendy Wayne, Esq., Massachusetts Committee for Public Counsel Services, for her assistance with immigration issues discussed in this chapter.

Endnotes

1. *See* Young, Nancy K., Sidney L. Gardner and Kimberly Dennis. *Responding to Alcohol and Other Drug Problems in Child Welfare: Weaving Together Practice and Policy.* Washington, D.C.: CWLA Press, 1998 (citing studies showing that drug use and abuse are a factor in 40-80% of child welfare cases, and estimating that substance use and abuse is a factor in 75% of all out-of-home placements).

2. *See* ABA Model Rule of Professional Conduct 1.6.

3. The Substance Abuse and Mental Health Services Administration (SAMHSA) of the U.S. Department of Health and Human Services has a "Substance Abuse Treatment Facility Locator" that identifies local programs by city and zip code. The locator is available at http://dasis3.samhsa.gov.

4. *See, e.g.,* www.mass.gov/dph/bsas/bsas.htm.

5. *See* D'Aunno, Lisa and Gay Chisum. "Parental Substance Abuse and Permanency Decision Making: Measuring Progress in Substance Abuse Recovery." *Children's Legal Rights Journal* 18, Fall 1998, 52, 53.

6. *See* 42 U.S.C. § 675(5)(C).

7. ASFA provides that, when a child has been in foster care for 15 of the last 22 months, the agency "shall file a petition to terminate the parental rights of the child's parents" unless the child is being cared for by a relative, the state has documented a "compelling reason for determining that filing such a petition would not be in the best interests of the child," or the state has not made the reasonable efforts necessary to achieve the goal of the case plan where the goal is reunification. 42 U.S.C. § 675(5)(E).

8. *See, e.g.,* Commonwealth v. Johnson, 59 Mass. App. Ct. 164, 167-68 (2003) (urine screen that stated on its face that "[a] second test must be used to obtain a confirmed analytical result" was not sufficiently reliable to be admitted under the medical records statute).

9. *See* 42 U.S.C. § 290dd-2; 42 C.F.R. §§ 2.1-2.67.

10. *See, e.g.,* In re Brianna B., 614 N.W.2d 790 (Neb. Ct. App. 2000) (evidence insufficient to show that father's alcohol use harmed children); Adoption of Katharine, 42 Mass. App. Ct. 25, 31 (1997) (findings did not establish nexus between mother's cocaine use and harm to the child).

11. *See* 42 U.S.C. § 671(a)(15); 45 C.F.R. § 1356.21(b).

12. *See, e.g.,* Care and Protection of Elaine, 54 Mass. App. Ct. 266, 274 (2002). Your father client may have disabilities recognized under the Americans with Disabilities Act (ADA), 42 U.S.C. § 12132 (1994). Such disabilities include certain mental illnesses, as well as substance addiction. *See* 42 U.S.C. § 12102(2). In many states, failure to provide the parent with appropriate services as required by the ADA is not a defense to a termination of parental rights proceeding. *See, e.g.,* In re Torrance P., 522 N.W.2d 243, 245-46 (Wis. Ct. App. 1994) ("Because the ADA does not affect our inquiry of whether [CPS] made a diligent effort to provide [the disabled father] with court-ordered services as required under [the state termination statute], we do not determine whether [CPS] reasonably accommodated [his] disability. That is a separate inquiry under the ADA, unrelated to the TPR proceedings. . . . [The father] may have a separate cause of action under the ADA based on [CPS's] actions or inactions; such a claim, however, is not a basis to attack the TPR order."); Adoption of Gregory, 434 Mass. 117, 122 (2001) ("If a parent believes that the department is not reasonably accommodating a disability, the parent should claim a violation of his rights under either the ADA or other antidiscrimination legislation, either when the parenting plan is adopted, when he receives those services, or shortly thereafter. . . . However, where, as here, a disabled parent fails to make a timely claim that the department is providing inadequate services for his needs, he may not raise noncompliance with the ADA or other antidiscrimination laws for the first time at a termination proceeding."). *But see* In re C.M., 526 N.W.2d 562, 566 (Iowa Ct. App. 1994) (suggesting that ADA applies to termination proceeding); In re Angel B., 659 A.2d 277, 279 (Me. 1995) (same). *See generally,* Glennon, Theresa. "Symposium: Lawyering for the Mentally Ill: Walking with Them: Advocating for Parents with Mental Illnesses in the Child Welfare System." *Temple Political & Civil Rights Law Review* 12, Spring 2003, 273; Mosier, Teri. Note, "Trying to Cure a Seven-Year Itch: The ADA Defense in Termination of Parental Rights Actions." *Brandeis Law Journal* 37, Summer 1998-99, 785. You must therefore identify the appropriate services, and CPS's failure to provide those services, well before trial.

13. *See* ABA Model Rule of Professional Conduct 1.14; ABA Standards of Practice for Attorneys Representing Parents in Abuse and Neglect Cases, Standard 18 ("Be aware of the client's mental health status and be prepared to assess whether the parent can assist with the case."), and Standard 18, commentary ("Attorneys representing parents must be able to determine whether a client's mental status (including mental illness and mental retardation) interferes with the client's ability to make decisions about the case.").

14. *See* ABA Model R. Prof. C. 1.14, Comment [6]; Renne, Jennifer. "Diminished Capacity." In *Representing Children in Child Protective Proceedings: Ethical and Practical Dimensions.* Albany, NY: LexisNexis, 2001, 4-5.

15. ABA Model R. Prof. C. 1.14(a).

16. *See* Renne, 2001, 4.

17. ABA Model R. Prof. C. 1.14., Comment [1].

18. If your father client's ability to make adequately considered decisions is impaired and you reasonably believe him to be at substantial risk of harm (physical, mental, financial or other), you may take steps to protect him, even to the extent of disclosing confidential information. *See* ABA Model R. Prof. C. 1.14(c). You may "consult[] with individuals or

entities that have the ability to take action to protect the client and, in appropriate cases, seek[] the appointment of a guardian ad litem, conservator or guardian." ABA Model R. Prof. C. 1.14(b). Any such actions must be "least intrusive" to the client. For example, you may, to protect the father, divulge confidences to his mother who cares for him, but not to CPS or relatives vying for placement of the child.

19. ABA Model R. Prof. C. 1.14(b). In at least one state, judges must consider a GAL appointment for a parent alleged by the agency to be unfit because of mental illness, retardation or other mental impairment. *See* N.C. Gen. Stat. § 7B-1101(1) ("a guardian *ad litem* shall be appointed in accordance with the provisions of G.S. 1A-1, Rule 17, to represent a parent . . . (1) where it is alleged that a parent's rights should be terminated pursuant to G.S. 7B-1111[a](6), and the incapability to provide proper care and supervision pursuant to that provision is the result of substance abuse, mental retardation, mental illness, organic brain syndrome, or another similar cause or condition.").

20. In some states, presence of a mental illness is not sufficient to show unfitness; the illness must affect the parent's ability to meet the child's needs or cause him to abuse or neglect the child. *See, e.g.,* Adoption of Eduardo, 57 Mass. App. Ct. 278, 282-83 (2003).

21. *Cf.* In re Adoption/Guardianship Nos. J9610436 and J9711031, 368 Md. 666, 796 A.2d 778, 787 (App. Ct. 2002) (reversing termination decree because child protection agency never offered father any "specialized services designed to be particularly helpful to a parent with [his] intellectual and cognitive skill levels," even though such services were available).

22. Domestic violence may play a part in one-third to one-half of child welfare cases. *See* Goodmark, Leigh. *Reasonable Efforts Checklist for Dependency Cases Involving Domestic Violence.* Reno: NV: National Council of Juvenile and Family Court Judges, 2008, 10 (citing Melanie Shepard and Michael Raschick). "How Child Welfare Workers Assess and Intervene around Issues of Domestic Violence." *Child Maltreatment* 4, 1999, 148, 149.

Domestic violence may be physical, sexual, emotional or psychological. Physical abuse may be blatant and obvious, such as bruises or broken bones, or it may be less visible. The abuser may push the victim against the wall, throw objects at her, or threaten to hit her. While most perpetrators of abuse are men and most victims are women, these roles are occasionally reversed.

23. *See* Quirion, Pauline. "Why Attorneys Should Routinely Screen Clients for Domestic Violence." *Boston Bar Journal* 42, Sept./Oct. 1998, 12.

24. *See* Goodmark, Leigh. "When a Parent is a Batterer: Understanding and Working with Abusive Fathers." *ABA Child Law Practice* 22(8), October 2003, 121, 126.

25. Ibid.

26. Even if CPS does not require an evaluation, the court may. Judges are increasingly aware of domestic violence issues, and many require evaluations to assess the risk perpetrators pose to children and partners. *See generally,* Goodmark, 2008; Dalton, Clare, Leslie Drozd and Frances Wong. *Navigating Custody and Visitation Evaluations in Cases with Domestic Violence: A Judge's Guide.* Reno, NV: National Council of Juvenile and Family Court Judges, 2004, rev. 2006.

27. For a selection of batterer's treatment programs and a discussion of the nature of treatment, *see* Child Welfare Information Gateway, *Batterer Intervention Programs,* available at www.childwelfare.gov/systemwide/service_array/domviolence/treatment/intervention.cfm. There is little research on the effectiveness of such programs, and some scholars believe they are of limited benefit in reducing family violence. *See* Babcock, Julia C., Charles E. Green and Chet Robie. "Does Batterers' Treatment Work? A Meta-Analytic

Review of Domestic Violence Treatment." *Clinical Psychology Review* 23(8), January 2004, 1023-1053 (concluding that current batterer's treatment programs "have a minimal impact on reducing recidivism beyond the effect of being arrested.").

Note that anger management classes are not the same as batterer's treatment, and are not considered appropriate for batterers. *See* Goodmark, Leigh. "Treatment Options for Batterers." In "A Balanced Approach to Handling Domestic Violence in Child Welfare Cases." *ABA Child Law Practice* 20(5), July 2001, 54. Family mediation and couples counseling are likewise inappropriate, because they subject the victim to greater risk of abuse. *See* Saunders, Daniel G. "Child Custody Decisions in Families Experiencing Woman Abuse." *Social Work* 39(1), January 1994, 51, 55.

28. *See, e.g.,* Custody of Vaughn, 422 Mass. 590, 599-600 (1996). The National Council of Juvenile and Family Court Judges has long advocated for a presumption against giving custody to the battering spouse. *See* National Council of Juvenile and Family Court Judges. Model Code on Domestic and Family Violence, § 401, 1994, 33.

29. The evidence might support an argument that the children were not harmed if they did not witness the abuse. *See, e.g.,* In re C.A.S., 828 A.2d 184 (D.C. 2003). But in most cases, the children will have witnessed it or will have witnessed the effects of it.

30. Children may be injured or killed in an assault by the batterer on the mother. *See* Quirion, Pauline, et al. "Protecting Children Exposed to Domestic Violence in Contested Custody and Visitation Litigation," *Boston University Public Interest Law Journal* 6, Winter 1997, 501, 509-10 & nn. 58-60, and studies cited therein. Many are injured when they try to intervene to protect the victim from the batterer's rampage. *See generally,* Roy, Maria. *Children in the Crossfire.* Deerfield Beach, FL: Health Communications, 1988, 89-90. Further, exposure to assaultive behavior traumatizes children and negatively impacts their mental health and development in many ways. *See* Quirion et al., 1997, 511-12, and studies cited therein. Even a single episode of violence can produce post-traumatic stress disorder in children. *See* Saunders, 1994, 52, and studies cited therein.

31. There are several resources available online. The ABA Commission on Immigration has a state-by-state locator for free and low-cost immigration legal assistance, available at www.abanet.org/publicserv/immigration/legal_services_directory_map.shtml. Other resources include the American Immigration Lawyers Association (www.aila.org), and the Immigrant Legal Resource Center (www.ilrc.org).

32. *See* Goodmark, Leigh. "Domestic Violence and Child Maltreatment in Immigrant Communities." *ABA Child Law Practice* 22(4), June 2003, 53, 62. *See generally,* Yali Lincroft et al. *Undercounted, Underserved: Immigrant and Refugee Families in the Child Welfare System.* Baltimore, MD: Annie E. Casey Foundation, 2006, available at www.f2f.ca.gov/res/pdf/UndercountedUnderserved.pdf.

33. Nonimmigrant visas are for temporary visitors to the United States. For more information, *see* the U.S. Department of State Web site at http://travel.state.gov/visa/temp/temp_1305.html.

34. 8 C.F.R. § 287.7.

35. *See, e.g.,* 8 U.S.C. §§ 1182 and 1227 (detailing grounds for inadmissibility and deportability).

CHAPTER SEVEN

Legal Strategies to Address Child Support Obligations

Daniel L. Hatcher

Legal Strategies to Address Child Support Obligations

Request that the court or agency not refer the father to child support enforcement services when reunification may be a goal.

➤ Argue that under federal law it is within the state's discretion to recover child support in child welfare cases.

➤ Argue that the state should exercise this discretion when it conflicts with case-planning goals relating to reunification.

➤ State that to do otherwise would be contrary to the child's best interest.

Argue that agency case plans cannot be derailed by imposing child support recovery mechanisms.

➤ Argue that if reunification with the father is a goal, pursing a government-owed debt directly conflicts with federal law regarding agency efforts to provide reunification services.

Combat any attempts by the state to terminate a father's rights based on his failure to pay child support.

➤ Argue that this would unconstitutionally deprive the father of his due process right to the care, custody, and control of his child.

Identify other legal strategies to oppose collecting child support.

➤ Oppose the amount of the child support order because it conflicts with case-planning goals or the child's best interest.

➤ Challenge the assignment of child support rights to the government as an involuntary assignment by the child to the state.

➤ Raise concerns under the Administrative Procedures Act in state-funded child welfare cases where the government continues to collect child support to reimburse its costs, even if there is no federal provision supporting it.

Download this and other checklists at **www.fatherhoodqic.org/checklists**

Case Scenario

Your father client hopes to reunify with his child and has started a reunification plan. Although he was unemployed and homeless, he just got a job driving a taxi and is saving money for a deposit on an apartment. A child support obligation was initiated when the child entered foster care, however, so the father's license was suspended due to lack of payment. His job is at risk, and 65 percent of his last paycheck was garnished for the child support debt. The apartment complex manager tells him his credit looks bad because of the unpaid child support debt and his application will likely be denied. The caseworker updates the reunification plan to require the father to pay $5,000 in child support arrearages in addition to current payments of $200 per month. The caseworker explains that if he does not make sufficient progress on the reunfication plan within the next six months the plan will change to termination of parental rights based on failure to obtain housing and provide adequate child support. As his lawyer, what can you do?

The legal and practical issues surrounding child support obligations have enormous impact on families in the child welfare system.[1] Unfortunately, these issues are often ignored, overlooked, or misunderstood. Efforts to engage nonresident fathers in the child welfare system are underway,[2] but those efforts will often be derailed if child support is not properly addressed. This chapter examines legal and policy concerns regarding child support enforcement in child welfare cases and shares legal strategies to address those concerns. While aimed at advocates for nonresident fathers, this chapter should also benefit advocates for custodial parents and for children as child support issues affect all parties in the child welfare system.

Understanding Child Support in Child Welfare Cases

Child support is crucial for low-income families. When the support amount is realistic and payments are directed to the custodial families, child support can help struggling single mothers lift their families from poverty and can improve family relationships with nonresident fathers. However, in the context of child welfare cases, the potential benefits of child support often turn to harm.

In the child welfare system, child support is not owed to the children. For children eligible for Title IV-E foster care assistance, federal law requires state child welfare agencies to enforce child support obligations against the parents. The payments do not benefit the children, but are rerouted to the state and federal government to reimburse the government costs of providing foster care assistance.

This cost-recovery effort can often derail case-planning goals, burdening already impoverished parents with added troubles that hamper reunification and undermine agency efforts to improve family relationships. Also, imposing government-owed child support obligations limits nonresident parents from providing informal and in-kind support to their children. Several state practices are legally questionable, at best, but legal strategies exist to challenge these practices.

> "A lot of guys, you know, they don't spend time with their kids because they don't have the money they think they need...whereas the child probably just wants to spend that time at the park, you know? Time at the park running around or something."
>
> —*Nonresident father*

Cost-recovery framework

Title IV-E of the Social Security Act, the largest source of federal funding for child welfare services, requires child welfare agencies to pursue child support obligations.[3] When children are "IV-E eligible,"[4] federal law requires child welfare agencies to seek child support "where appropriate" by referring cases for child support enforcement services. Resulting payments are generally kept by the government to reimburse the costs of foster care.[5] In state-funded child welfare cases (where children are not IV-E eligible), no federal requirement to pursue child support exists. Nonetheless, states often pursue child support in such cases despite the lack of a federal requirement.

Consequences of child support cost-recovery efforts

The two primary goals of the child welfare system are protecting the interests of children and strengthening and preserving families. Although the Adoption and Safe Families Act increased the focus on adoption, providing services to parents to encourage reunification continues as a core goal. The child support cost-recovery efforts divert attention from the agency's mission, and often conflict with case-planning goals. As a low-income parent struggles to meet reunification plan requirements, imposing a government-owed child support obligation can derail the parent's efforts through immediate enforcement mechanisms, such as suspending licenses, garnishing wages, and credit reporting.

For nonresident fathers, the harm child support cost-recovery efforts cause can be significant. Historically, child welfare agencies have not done well reaching out to nonresident fathers. Recently, the child welfare system has begun recognizing the need to engage nonresident fathers to encourage increased involvement in their children's lives and possible reunification in appropriate cases. However, if the initial contact with a father is to force him into court for a child support obligation that is owed to the government (rather than his children) and that he likely cannot afford to pay, coupled with contempt proceedings, driver's license suspension, and garnishment of up to 65 percent of his wages, the engagement effort will be thwarted. The father will further retreat from involvement with the agency—and his family—and his efforts to comply with case planning requirements will be severely hampered.

Legal Strategies to Address Child Support Concerns

As a lawyer representing nonresident fathers, you have several legal strategies to address concerns about child support enforcement in child welfare cases.[6]

Discretion not to initiate child support

The federal law triggering the child support cost-recovery requirement in child welfare cases also includes discretion. The law provides that "where appropriate," states should "secure an assignment" of child support rights for children receiving IV-E foster care maintenance payments.[7] Federal guidance interprets the statutory language as providing states flexibility in determining that certain child welfare cases are not appropriate for initiating child support enforcement actions.[8] The guidance explains that states should decide a case "on an individual basis, considering the best interests of the child and the circumstances of the family," and the guidance suggests considering whether initiating the government-owed child support obligation would be a barrier to reunification.[9]

Some states, like California and Ohio, have state statutes that require exercising discretion before referring a case for child support enforcement services.[10] However, many states either have no legislation or policies implementing the discretion, or require initiating child support obligations in all cases. Nonetheless, even in a state where no discretion is provided in state statute or regulation, you can still argue for the exercise of discretion under federal law. In any case where

■ Resources

➤ Federal guidance regarding discretion to not refer child
welfare cases for child support enforcement services:
www.acf.hhs.gov/j2ee/programs/cb/laws_policies/laws/cwpm/policy_dsp.jsp?
citID=170

➤ Federal communication regarding coordination
between child welfare and child support agencies:
www.acf.hhs.gov/programs/cb/laws_policies/policy/im/2007/im0706.pdf

➤ Daniel L. Hatcher. "Collateral Children: Consequence and
Illegality at the Intersection of Foster Care and Child Support."
Brooklyn Law Review 74(4), 2009, available at
http://papers.ssrn.com/sol3/papers.cfm?abstract_id=1424485

reunification is a possible goal, you can argue that either the agencies or the courts
should exercise this discretion under federal law and find a referral for child support enforcement services inappropriate because it conflicts with case planning
goals.[11] Supporting the argument is the simple principle that agencies and courts
must ensure every action regarding children in the child welfare system is in the
best interests of the child.

Conflicts with reunification requirements and illegal case plans

If you cannot convince the child welfare agency or the court to exercise discretion and decide that initiating child support is inappropriate, another legal challenge may be possible. With some specific exceptions, federal law requires child
welfare agencies to make "reasonable efforts" in order "to preserve and reunify
families."[12] Case plans must incorporate these reunification services,[13] and a "case
review system" is required to regularly review progress toward meeting the case
plan goals.[14] Thus, if reunification is a possible goal in a child welfare case, you
can argue that pursuing a government-owed child support obligation directly
conflicts with federal law and regulations requiring reunification services. Imposing a debt owed to the government upon an already impoverished parent will
directly hamper the parent's efforts to become economically stable to reunify with
his child.

Also, in several states, child welfare agencies include the child support obligations as part of the federally required case plans (e.g., a reunification plan might require the parent to pay regular child support to the government to comply with the plan). Adding government-owed debt collection efforts to case plans required by federal law to assist in reunification efforts arguably conflicts with the federal requirements and is therefore illegal.

Unconstitutional grounds for terminating parental rights

In many states, the statutory grounds for terminating parental rights consider the failure to pay the government-owed child support obligation as a factor. Some states specifically allow that factor alone to warrant termination.[15] Although a parent's failure to support a child may initially seem relevant to the decision to terminate parental rights, in child welfare cases the support obligation is not owed to the child. Including the cost-recovery debt as grounds to terminate parental rights subverts the child welfare mission and the overarching consideration in termination proceedings—the best interests of the child.

If you face these circumstances, you can argue that terminating parental rights for a government-owed debt is unconstitutional on substantive due process grounds.[16] The interests of parents and children in the parent-child relationship are constitutionally protected. The substantive due process heightened scrutiny forbids the government from infringing on such fundamental liberty interests, "unless the infringement is narrowly tailored to serve a compelling state interest."[17] The compelling state interest in termination of parental rights proceedings is protecting the welfare of children. A statute that allows ending the parent-child relationship because of a government-owed debt is not narrowly tailored or even related to that compelling interest.

Additional strategies

In addition to the legal issues briefly described above, other legal strategies exist. For example, if a court disregards arguments against initiating child support, you can still direct your advocacy toward the amount of the order. In most if not all state child support guidelines, grounds for deviating from the statutorily suggested guidelines amount are available. You can argue that a court should deviate downward from the guidelines in child welfare cases based upon best interests grounds and conflict with case-planning goals.

Additionally, you may be able to challenge the actual assignment of child support rights to the government. An assignment is a form of contract, and the forced assignment (often by state statute) of child support rights without voluntary agreement is legally questionable. Some states have no provision to start the assignment; rather they simply consider the child support as owed to the government with no legal process for the transfer of rights.

Finally, in state-funded child welfare cases (for children who are not IV-E eligible), there is no federal provision for collecting child support to reimburse government costs. Nonetheless, many states still pursue child support in these cases and keep the resulting collections. The asserted basis for the cost-recovery collections in state-funded cases is a patchwork of informal federal agency communications, therefore raising Administrative Procedures Act (APA) concerns.[18]

Conclusion

Child support issues facing nonresident fathers (and all parties) in child welfare cases are often overlooked and warrant serious attention by advocates. Because your state's agencies, courts, and legislatures have likely not grappled with these issues, education is a key part of your advocacy strategies. Although the legal issues can become complex, the core themes are simple. Child support should not harm children or conflict with case-planning goals, and all actions by child welfare agencies and the courts should be guided by the best interests of the child standard—not the government's fiscal interests in cost recovery.

Endnotes

1. For a more detailed analysis of the issues addressed in this chapter, *see* Daniel L. Hatcher. "Collateral Children: Consequence and Illegality at the Intersection of Foster Care and Child Support." *Brooklyn Law Review* 74(4), 2009, available at http://papers.ssrn.com/sol3/papers.cfm?abstract_id=1424485.

2. For simplicity, this chapter refers to custodial parents as mothers and noncustodial parents as fathers or nonresident fathers.

3. 42 U.S.C. § 671(a)(17).

4. The specific IV-E eligibility requirements are complicated, but primarily focus on limiting the federal assistance for children removed from low-income families that would have been eligible for welfare assistance. *See* 42 U.S.C.A. § 670; 42 U.S.C.A. § 672.

5. 42 U.S.C. § 671(a)(17).

6. For additional analysis regarding these strategies, *see* Hatcher, "Collateral Children," 2009.

7. 42 U.S.C. § 671(a)(17).

8. U.S. Department of Health and Human Services, Administration for Children & Families, Child Welfare Policy Manual, 8.4C Title IV-E, General Title IV-E Requirements, Child support, available at www.acf.hhs.gov/j2ee/programs/cb/laws_policies/laws/cwpm/policy_dsp.jsp?citID=170.

9. Ibid. Many other circumstances might warrant discretion to not initiate child support obligations. For example, even where reunification is not a goal, a parent may be very involved in the child's life—with visitations, informal support, providing child care, etc. so that imposing government-owed support may harm the relationship.

10. Ohio Rev. Code Ann. § 2151.361; Cal. Fam. Code § 17552.

11. Even if reunification is not the goal, discretionary arguments are still possible—such as arguing the referral would conflict with family relations and the best interests of the child, or might pose an undue hardship based upon disability.

12. 42 U.S.C. § 671(a)(15).

13. 42 U.S.C.A. § 675(1)(b); 45 C.F.R. § 1356.21(b) & (g)(4).

14. 42 U.S.C.A. § 675(5); 42 U.S.C.A. § 671(a)(16).

15. *E.g.*, N.C.G.S.A. § 7B-1111(a)(3).

16. Additional arguments may exist, such as a possible violation of the Cruel and Unusual Punishment Clause. For further analysis of the arguments, *see* Hatcher, "Collateral Children," 2009.

17. Reno v. Flores, 507 U.S. 292, 301-302 (1993).

18. For additional analysis regarding these possible arguments, *see* Hatcher, "Collateral Children," 2009.

CHAPTER EIGHT

Representing Incarcerated Nonresident Fathers in Child Welfare Cases

Kathleen Creamer

CHECKLIST

Representing Incarcerated Nonresident Fathers in Child Welfare Cases

Know the Adoption and Safe Families Act's timeframes and how they may impact your client.

➤ Be aware of the requirement to terminate parental rights if children have been in foster care for 15 of the last 22 months *and the relevant exceptions.*

Learn laws regarding the father's rights to participate in hearings and visitation, and incarceration as a basis to terminate parental rights.

By regular in-person and written communication, guide the father through the process, ensuring he has established goals and understands the steps he can take to accomplish them. Encourage your client to:

➤ Take part in programming offered at the correctional facility that will help him fulfill his case plan and reach his goals (e.g., parenting classes; job training; drug, alcohol or mental health services).

➤ Communicate regularly with the child welfare agency. (Determine if the father has a social worker in his facility who can help him communicate with the agency.)

➤ Help your client reach out to his children in any way possible. (Ensure your client has access to pens, papers, envelopes, and stamps and learn the facility's rules about phone use.)

Work with the child welfare agency to involve the father in permanency planning and to establish case plan goals for him.

File written motions, if necessary, to ensure your client can appear in person (or by phone or video conferencing) at hearings. Ensure he can appear in plainclothes and unshackled.

Ensure visitation occurs in some form.

➤ Consider virtual visits through teleconferencing or by videotape when in-person contact is not possible.

➤ Work with the jail to arrange appropriate visitation.

➤ Present evidence about the visitation conditions at the father's facility as part of your advocacy for visitation (Is it possible to visit in a family visitation room or outside? Can the father not be shackled?)

If reunification cannot be achieved due to time constraints or the father does not desire it, counsel the father on other permanency options and their legal effects.

Download this and other checklists at **www.fatherhoodqic.org/checklists**

If you are appointed to represent an incarcerated nonresident father, you will likely face some common challenges: no one may know where the father is located, everyone is suspicious of his past criminal activity, and no one is quite sure where he fits into his child's life. To further complicate things, research shows that when a child enters foster care, social workers often engage in little outreach to nonresident fathers and make little effort to include them in case planning for their children.[1] The reality is that not only do these fathers have legal rights worth defending, they have the potential to contribute to their children's lives.[2]

Many fathers may themselves be viable permanency resources for their children. They may also connect their children to other permanency resources, such as paternal relatives, and can provide valuable information about the child's health, education, and family history. It can be important for a child in foster care to know she has a parent who cares about her, even if he can't be a placement option. The child welfare system must recognize the valuable role incarcerated fathers can play in their children's lives. Your legal representation is critical to ensure the father is given a voice and a role in his child's permanency planning.

This chapter shares key legal issues that arise when representing nonresident incarcerated fathers in child welfare cases and effective representation strategies.

Identifying Key Legal Issues

As the number of incarcerated fathers nationwide rises dramatically,[3] the child welfare system struggles to resolve the rights and responsibilities of these fathers. The enactment of the Adoption and Safe Families Act (ASFA), and with it the requirement that the state move to terminate parental rights once children have been in foster care for 15 of the last 22 months,[4] has raised numerous questions about the rights of incarcerated parents, particularly those whose sentences may exceed 15 months.[5]

At all times during the case, be aware of the ASFA timeframes and how they may impact your client. Pay special attention to the exceptions to the 15 of 22 month rule.[6] Because the father may avoid termination of parental rights when his children are residing with family members,[7] explore early on and throughout the case any viable relative placements for the children. Also make sure you know the law in your jurisdiction,[8] particularly how it addresses such controversial issues as:

- **Does the incarcerated father have the right to be physically present at hearings?** If not, does he have the right to participate in these proceedings by phone?[9] Does this right attach at all phases of the child welfare case, or only at the termination of parental rights phase? Most jurisdictions require some opportunity for the parent to meaningfully participate in his hearings.[10] However, some have held that phone participation is sufficient,[11] while others have held that no presence is required so long as the client is represented by counsel.[12]

- **Does the incarcerated father have a right to visit with the child at his detention facility?** If there is no absolute right to visitation, what factors must the court consider in deciding whether to permit visitation? Many jurisdictions use a "best interest of the child" standard to determine whether to permit visitation in prison,[13] while others will not deny visitation without an affirmative showing of harm to the child.[14]

- **Will incarceration alone be sufficient to terminate parental rights (TPR)?** Most states have TPR statutes that address parental incarceration.[15] In many jurisdictions, a parent's incarceration is itself a ground for termination, particularly where the parent is facing a lengthy sentence.[16] In others, it is a factor that may be considered along with its impact on the parent-child relationship.[17] A few jurisdictions relax the ASFA requirement that termination petitions be filed when a child has been in care for 15 of the last 22 months when a parent is incarcerated.[18]

Ensuring Meaningful Client Participation in the Case

Attorney-client communication

Given the significant legal challenges facing the incarcerated father, regular attorney-client communication and planning is critical. Ensuring regular communication may be challenging when the father is frequently moved from facility to facility, or he is located far from the courthouse.[19] Locating a client in the prison population may also prove difficult, although several local and state jurisdictions and the Federal Bureau of Prisons have online inmate locators.[20] These locators should reveal the father's location and his assigned inmate number. Because detention facilities use these numbers rather than names to identify inmates, be sure to include the inmate number on all communications with the father and prison staff.

Assessing Case Plan Supports

The detention facility where your client is incarcerated is a valuable partner in case planning efforts. Be sure you know what regulations and resources the detention facility has to support case planning, including:

➤ Does the facility offer parenting programming? Marriage/relationship classes? GED programming? Job training?

➤ Does the facility offer drug/alcohol treatment? Mental health treatment?

➤ How can the father access available programming? Is there a waiting list?

➤ Is the father assigned a social worker at the facility? Is that social worker available to help him communicate with the child welfare agency and his attorney?

➤ Will the father be able to send mail? How can he obtain paper, pens, envelopes and stamps?

➤ What are the phone regulations? How often can the father use the phone? Who may he call? Who pays for phone calls?

With regular in-person and written communication, you can coach your client through the child welfare process, ensuring he is aware of his case plan goals and what steps he can take during incarceration to meet these goals.[21] Often resources to meet some permanency plan goals, such as parenting education or drug treatment, are available at the correctional facility and you should encourage your client to take advantage of such programming. Also encourage your client to communicate regularly with the child welfare agency and reach out to his child in any way possible. Counsel your client throughout the dependency process to ensure he understands the court proceedings and his legal options. In cases where reunification cannot be reasonably achieved within the statutory timeframe or is not the father's preference, counsel the father on other permanency options and their legal effects. These options may include voluntary relinquishment and adoption, guardianship by paternal kin or, in some jurisdictions, open adoption with ongoing contact.

Participating in court proceedings

Your role includes making diligent efforts to ensure your client has an opportunity to meaningfully participate in court proceedings. This includes arranging for your client to participate in person at every hearing by filing any necessary written motions.[22] Where in-person participation is prohibited by the court or the detention facility, try to arrange alternatives, such as audio or video conferencing. Also take steps to ensure your client can appear at the hearing in plainclothes rather than a uniform and shackles.

You will need to fully prepare your client to participate in the hearing. Explain the purpose of the hearing, what requests or recommendations the other parties are likely to make, and what issues the judge will have to resolve. The father should be prepared to respond to questions concerning his relationship with his child and what role he hopes to play in his child's permanency plan, as well as questions related to his sentence and his plans upon release. After the hearing, explain in writing what the court ordered, when the next hearing is, the purpose of the next hearing, and what steps he should take in the interim.

Participating in case planning

The incarcerated father has the right to be included in all planning for his child. Often the child welfare agency neglects to ensure the father participates in this planning and does not clearly instruct him about the goals he must reach to reunify with his child.[23] Ask the child welfare agency to involve you and the father in all planning meetings about the child. The father should have the opportunity to collaborate with the child welfare agency to determine what goal is appropriate for his child. If the father does not seek to reunify with his child, he still may be able to help plan for his child. For example, he may be able to suggest paternal relatives as placement resources for the child, or help link the child to other relatives or family friends for support. Additionally, the father may provide valuable input into the needs of the child and can help determine what sorts of educational, therapeutic, or medical supports may be appropriate.

Any case plan goals set for the father should be feasible and appropriate to his circumstances. Although few states have defined the agency's reasonable efforts obligation for incarcerated parents,[24] few permit the reasonable efforts requirement to be waived based on parental incarceration.[25] The case plan should state clear goals for the father and explain what efforts the child welfare agency will make to assist him. For instance, if the case plan calls for written communication between father and child, ask the agency to ensure the father has paper, envelopes, and stamps. If the case plan calls for visitation, the agency should detail who is responsible for transportation and how frequently visits will occur.

Assessing Visitation Conditions

The father's attorney should contact or, if possible, visit the detention facility to obtain answers to these questions:

➤ Are touch visits permitted, or will the child have to visit through a plexiglass wall?

➤ Will the father have to remain shackled during the visit?

➤ What kind of security is present? What will the child experience going through security?

➤ Who may supervise the visit?

➤ How child-friendly are the visitation accommodations (e.g., Are the walls colorful or decorated? Are there toys, books, or child-sized furniture?)

➤ Is there a special family visitation room?

➤ Is it possible to visit outside?

➤ Are there toys or activities for the child?

Facilitating Contact

Especially when reunification is the case plan goal, regular visitation is key to maintaining and improving the relationship between the father and child.[26] Although many jurisdictions permit and even encourage visitation at the father's jail or prison, concerns surround sending children to detention facilities. In particular, child welfare agencies and children's attorneys often fear visitation may harm the child's physical or emotional safety.

It is therefore important to advocate vigorously for visitation. Address visitation concerns directly by gathering and presenting evidence about the visitation conditions at the father's detention facility. Visitation conditions vary widely and many detention facilities try to ensure visitation is a child-friendly and positive experience. Concerns may be alleviated by thoroughly investigating and sharing a facility's visitation conditions.

If the court prohibits visitation, explore any other resources available to ensure ongoing contact between the father and child. A growing number of detention facilities offer virtual visitation, which allows the father and child to visit by videoconferencing. Others allow parents to create and send a video or audiotape of themselves reading or talking to the child. Additionally, e-mail access is being

Resources

➤ **National Resource Center on Children and Families of the Incarcerated**
www.fcnetwork.org/
Includes an "incarcerated fathers library," a searchable database of national and state programs providing assistance to children of offenders, and a wealth of other resources.

➤ **Center for Children of Incarcerated Parents**
www.e-ccip.org/index.html
Offers publications for parents and advocates, research on children of incarcerated parents, and other useful information.

➤ **National Resource Center for Family-Centered Practice and Permanency Planning**
Children of Incarcerated Parents Web site: www.hunter.cuny.edu/socwork/nrcfcpp/info_services/children-of-incarcerated-parents.html
Includes links to dozens of resources, many specific to youth in foster care.

piloted by the Federal Bureau of Prisons and may be available in some state facilities as well.[27] It may help to contact the detention facility as well as a local prisoner services organization[28] to identify programs that ensure father-child contact.

Conclusion

Although representing an incarcerated nonresident father can be challenging, there is tremendous opportunity for legal advocacy to have a positive impact on the family. Your representation ensures the father is given a voice in his child's future, and the opportunity to forge a lifelong relationship with the child.

Endnotes

1. A study of 1,222 caseworkers in four states found that the child welfare agency failed to reach out to the nonresident father in almost 50% of cases in which children were placed in foster care. Malm K., J. Murray and R. Geen. *What About the Dads? Child Welfare Agencies' Efforts to Identify, Locate and Involve Nonresident Fathers*. Washington, D.C.: The Urban Institute, 2006.

2. Note that maintaining the parent-child relationship is of great long-term benefit to the father. Research shows that incarcerated men who assume parenting roles upon release have higher rates of post-release success. Hairston, C. Finney. "Prisoners and Families: Parenting Issues during Incarceration." Paper presented at the From Prison to Home conference, 2002, 43, available at www.urban.org/UploadedPDF/410628_PrisonersandFamilies.pdf.

3. From 1991 to 2007, the number of fathers in prison rose by 76%. Glaze, Lauren E. et al. "Parents in Prison and their Minor Children." *Bureau of Justice Statistics Special Report*. Washington, D.C.: U.S. Department of Justice, Office of Justice Programs, 2008, 2.

4. 42 U.S.C. § 675(5)(E).

5. "The requirement to file a termination petition has a special impact on incarcerated parents whose children are in foster care. For many of these parents, time will simply run out before they can complete their sentences." Hirsch, Amy, et al. *Every Door Closed: Barriers Facing Parents with Criminal Records*, 2002, 67, available at www.clasp.org/publications/every_door_closed.pdf.

6. 42 U.S.C.A. § 675 (5)(E) provides the following exceptions to the 15/22 month filing requirement: the child is being cared for by a relative, the existence of a compelling reason that termination would not be in the best interest of the child, and the failure of the state to provide reasonable efforts.

7. Ibid.

8. For an overview of state statutes regarding parental incarceration and ASFA, *see* Lee, Arlene et al. *The Impact of the Adoption and Safe Families Act on Children of Incarcerated Parents*. Washington, D.C.: Child Welfare League of America, 2005.

9. For a useful discussion of how courts approach due process and the right to participate, *see* Laver, Mimi. "Incarcerated Parents: What You Should Know When Handling an Abuse or Neglect Case." *ABA Child Law Practice* 20(10), December 2001, 145-146, 150-155.

10. Ibid., 146.

11. *See, e,g.,* In re A.P., 692 A.2d 240 (Pa. Super. Ct. 1997).

12. *See, e.g.,* In re J.L.D., 794 P.2d 319 (Kan. Ct. App. 1990); In re C.C.E., 540 S.E.2d 704 (Ga. Ct. App. 2000); In re Eric L. II v. Eric L. Sr., 2008 NY Slip Op. 4175 (App. Div. Dep't 2008).

13. *See, e.g.,* N.Y. Soc. Serv. Law § 384-b(7)(f)(2).

14. *See, e.g.,* In re J.N., 138 Cal. App. 4th 450, 500 (Ct. App. 2006) (it is error to deny visitation without showing of detriment to child); In re C.J., 729 A.2d 89, 95 (Pa. Super. Ct. 1999) (showing of grave threat required to suspend prison visitation).

15. Lee et al., 2005, 11.

16. Twenty-five states have statutes that permit termination based on the length of incarceration. Ibid.

17. *See* Ga. Code Ann. § 15-11-94(4)(B)(iii) (2008); 10 Okla. Stat. Ann. § 7006-1.1(A)(12)(2008); Or. Rev. Stat. § 419B.504(6)(2008).

18. *See* Colo. Rev. Stat. Ann. § 19-3-604(2)(k)(IV)(2008); Neb. Rev. Stat. §43-292.02(2)(b)(2007); N.M. Stat. Ann. § 32A-4-28(D)(2008).

19. Over 60% of parents in state prison and over 80% in federal prison are held more than 100 miles from their home. Mumola, Christopher J. *Incarcerated Parents and their Children. Bureau of Justice Statistics Special Report*. Washington, D.C.: U.S. Department of Justice, Office of Justice Programs, 2005.

20. *See, e.g.,* the Federal Bureau of Prisons Web site: www.bop.gov/iloc2/LocateInmate.jsp.

21. For an overview of the communication and representation obligations of parents' attorneys, *see* the *ABA Standards of Practice for Attorneys Representing Parents in Abuse and Neglect Cases*. Washington, D.C.: ABA Center on Children and the Law, 2006, available at www.abanet.org/child/clp/ParentStds.pdf.

22. The attorney should also be mindful that there may be costs to the father of being away from the jail, such as losing jail privileges. Ibid., 18.

23. "Fathers in Prison." *Best Practice, Next Practice: Family-Centered Child Welfare*, Summer 2002, 31, available at www.hunter.cuny.edu/socwork/nrcfcpp/downloads/newsletter/BPNPSummer02.pdf.

24. California is among the few states to describe required efforts for incarcerated parents, including visits, phone calls and transportation. Cal.Welf. & Inst. Code § 361.5(e)(1)(2008). *See also* N.Y. Soc. Serv. Law § 384-b(2)(b)(2008) (defining "incarcerated parent" as "parent" for terms of reasonable efforts requirement.)

25. Allard, Patricia and Lynn Lu. *Rebuilding Families, Changing Lives: State Obligations to Children in Foster Care and Their Incarcerated Parents*. New York: Brennan Center for Justice at NYU School of Law, 2006, 20, available at http://brennan.3cdn.net/a714f3bf3 bc8235faf_4am6b84bh.pdf. *But see* N.D. Cent. Code § 27-20-02 (3)(2007), defining parental incarceration as an aggravating circumstance, based on length of incarceration.

26. Margolies, Julie Kowitz and Tamar Kraft-Stolar. *When 'Free' Means Losing your Mother: The Collision of Child Welfare and the Incarceration of Women in New York State*. New York: Women in Prison Project, Correctional Association of New York, 2006, 19, available at www.correctionalassociation.org/publications/download/wipp/reports/When_Free_Rpt_Feb_2006.pdf.

27. *See, e.g.,* the Federal Bureau of Prisons Web site at www.bop.gov/inmate_programs/trulincs_faq.jsp#2.

28. *See, e.g.,* PB&J Family Services in New Mexico (www.pbjfamilyservices.org/index.html) and The Pennsylvania Prison Society (www.prisonsociety.org/index.shtml).

CHAPTER NINE

Addressing
Ethical Issues

Jennifer L. Renne

Addressing Ethical Issues

Remember, the appointment creates the attorney-client relationship.

➤ Even if the father's whereabouts are unknown, you must make reasonable efforts to locate him.

➤ If your client's paternity has not been established, following his wishes, request paternity testing immediately.

Competently represent your father client.

➤ Consult an experienced lawyer to gain expertise if you are new to the field.

➤ Address critical legal needs of your client:

    ➤ Establish paternity.

    ➤ Determine the place, frequency, and need for supervision of visits.

    ➤ Assess whether paternal relatives are capable of caring for the child if the father is unable.

Assess your options if you lose contact with your client. Consider:

    ➤ how much information you have gathered on the father's wishes before his absence;

    ➤ whether too much time has passed to determine if his previously expressed wishes are still accurate; and

    ➤ if circumstances have changed and you can't infer what his wishes may be.

Avoid representing multiple fathers or both parents in one case.

➤ Dual representation may result in a conflict of interest and prevent you from zealously pursuing both clients' objectives simultaneously.

Download this and other checklists at **www.fatherhoodqic.org/checklists**

A s you represent nonresident fathers in child welfare cases, you are likely to face challenging ethical issues. For example:

- When does your ethical and legal obligation to your client begin and end?
- How should you represent a father you haven't heard from in months?
- Can you represent two fathers in the same case?

This chapter focuses on these and other ethical issues by referencing the ABA Model Rules of Professional Conduct (MRs).[1]

Appointment

Many courts around the country still struggle with appointing qualified counsel for all parents, and the rate of appointment for nonresident fathers is dramatically low. One study cites that nonresident parents are appointed counsel approximately half as often as other clients.[2] Yet federally-supported research reveals that the participation and involvement of nonresident fathers improves outcomes. Even beyond outcomes, children deserve the opportunity to form relationships with their fathers.

A threshold ethical issue is whether mere appointment to a case establishes a lawyer/client relationship. Sometimes the court will appoint a lawyer to represent the parent(s) at the preliminary hearing.[3] What are the ethical considerations for a lawyer in the following circumstances?

1) The father's identity and contact information, including address is known, but the father is not present.
2) The father's identity is known, but his whereabouts are unknown.
3) The putative father is named on the petition, but paternity has not been established.
4) The father's identity is unknown.
5) There are multiple fathers for a sibling group (may a lawyer be appointed to represent all the fathers?)

Under the first two circumstances, when the father's identity and contact information is known, or identity is known but whereabouts are not, you can be appointed. However, unless and until contact is made, typically you may not assert any positions on behalf of the father. This is because the courts generally find that any action taken without the client's knowledge or consent cannot bind the client,[4] and may violate MR 1.2, which says the client, not the lawyer, controls the objectives of the representation.[5]

On the other hand, if you are appointed, you must make reasonable efforts to locate the father. If the father receives notice of the appointment, the court will assume the father had a reasonable expectation that the lawyer would represent him.[6] It is the appointment which triggers the ethical duties, including making an effort to locate the client,[7] explain the case, elicit the client's position,[8] and advocate for the client's position.[9] A lack of effort on your part may lead to discipline and/or a malpractice claim.[10] (See *Consequences for Failing to Adhere to Ethical Standards* box.)

To establish malpractice, the client must show harm. Failure to locate fathers early may prevent children from establishing a relationship with them, deprive children of potential paternal relative resources, or delay permanency (either reunification with father, relative placement, or adoption if the termination of parental rights process is delayed).

For the third circumstance (putative father is named, but paternity has not been established), you *may* be appointed, particularly if the putative father is present. In that instance, follow the client's wishes (and certainly a court order) regarding paternity testing. Good advice at this stage is critical to establishing paternal rights, if the client is interested in that objective.[11]

If the father's identity is unknown (#4 above), the ethics rules do not specifically prohibit the court from appointing a lawyer for the purpose of preserving procedural rights. However, any lawyer that would be appointed on behalf of an unnamed client is limited in terms of advocacy strategy and tactics because there is no client directing the litigation.[12]

The fifth and final circumstance (multiple fathers) is addressed in the "conflict of interest" section below.

For all of these circumstances, if there has been no contact, you may not advocate on behalf of the father. But the lack of contact does not mean that a lawyer/client relationship has not been established; the lawyer still owes the father ethical obligations, including the duty to attempt to locate him. Upon appointment, if the father is named but not present, make sure the court orders the agency to make a reasonable attempt to find the putative father, so the father will have the ability to be present, answer the petition, and be represented.

Competent Representation

MR 1.1 provides that competent representation includes the following key components:

- legal knowledge
- legal skill
- thoroughness
- preparation

Consequences for Not Following Ethical Standards

The most common result of failing to follow ethical standards is that a complaint or grievance is filed against a lawyer with Bar Counsel or other disciplinary board. Typically, grievance commissions do not find unethical conduct based upon a mistake or error in judgment. Unethical conduct means wrongdoing, a violation of a profession's code of ethics. Ethics violations can result in a range of sanctions from censure (public reprimand), temporary suspension, to disbarment.

A second consequence of unethical conduct is that a client may file for malpractice. A client must prove that: (1) a lawyer/client relationship exists, (2) a duty was breached, and (3) an injury occurred. Merely violating an ethical rule is not a basis for civil liability. However, violating a rule may be evidence used to support a civil claim because the lawyer has breached an applicable standard of conduct.

Finally, a lawyer may be found to have provided ineffective assistance of counsel. If state law establishes the right to counsel (for a TPR or dependency case), then the Sixth Amendment guarantee of effective assistance of counsel applies. To establish a constitutional violation, a client has to show: (1) deficient performance, and (2) prejudice.

Legal knowledge and skill

While ethics rules generally permit a lawyer with no prior experience to handle a particular type of case, the rules require that lawyer to develop competency, usually through association with a lawyer experienced in such matters.[13] The ABA Standards of Practice for Attorneys Representing Parents in Abuse and Neglect Cases lays out the wide range of topics that a lawyer must be familiar with before handling a dependency case.[14] Other chapters in this book describe additional training issues when representing nonresident fathers, such as protecting the client's standing, child support, and constitutional rights.

Thorough and reasonable preparation

Incompetent representation can result from inexperience, lack of training, or more commonly, procrastination and neglect of client matters. Upon appointment, immediately make reasonable efforts to locate your nonresident father client. Critical legal rights need to be explored and explained to the father as soon as possible. These include:

- establishing paternity if at issue;
- reviewing whether there are existing custody orders through domestic relations court that may affect the dependency case;
- determining visitation parameters (frequency, location, supervised versus unsupervised);
- determining whether paternal relatives can take physical or legal custody if the father is not in a position to do so;
- tracking an existing or a potential parallel criminal case associated with the abuse/neglect allegations; and
- explaining to the father the basic process of a dependency case, including ASFA timelines, the role of the child welfare agency, etc.

In addition to explaining basic rights and responsibilities to the father, encourage cooperation with the agency to the degree that the father is interested. *Even if the father is at first uninterested or ambivalent about gaining custody of the child, the lawyer needs to be involved early on in the case because case planning can (or at least should) begin immediately.* This establishes the father as a key player in the case, and the sooner he is involved in that process, the greater advantage he has if and when he decides he wants to work to gain custody and/or have regular contact with the child.

As the lawyer for the nonresident father, push to frontload services early in the case, including visitation, social, and rehabilitative services. Advocating for frontloading of services not only satisfies the MR 1.1 obligation to provide thorough and reasonably prepared representation, but also is consistent with your ethical obligation under MR 1.3 to provide diligent representation.

Diligent Representation and Maintaining Communication

When representing nonresident fathers, you may have difficulty maintaining contact with your client. MR 1.4 explicitly directs the lawyer to keep the client reasonably informed about the status of the case, promptly comply with reasonable requests for information, and explain the case to the extent reasonably necessary to permit the client to make informed decisions. MR 1.3 requires the lawyer to act with reasonable diligence and promptness in representing a client.

Explain to your client exactly what to expect in the court proceedings and work with him *regularly* to determine his goals. Recognize any bias you may have against fathers. For example, a common belief is that fathers are uninterested in seeking custody or unmotivated to do what is necessary to obtain custody.[15]

Diligent representation (MR 1.3) and the degree to which lawyers must maintain communication (MR 1.4) are subjective issues. Explain all the options, understand the father's goals, advise him accordingly, and work with the other parties to achieve them. The following tips will help ensure compliance with these ethics rules:

- If there is no preexisting custody order granting the mother sole custody, or if a preexisting domestic relations case order grants joint custody, then explore whether the agency made *reasonable efforts* to prevent the child's removal from the father, or whether reasonable efforts have been made to reunify with the father.

- If the father is not in a position or does not desire custody, *explore other rights* such as visitation, and advocate accordingly.

- Advise the father to *cooperate with the agency*. This may even involve concurrent planning. Understand how concurrent planning benefits parents (i.e., frontloading of services), and explain to fathers how to take advantage of the services.[16]

- Find out from the father if he has *relatives or other people who may be interested and suitable long- or short-term caregivers*. Do not rely on social services to do the legwork to investigate these people. If necessary, contact them directly.

- Participate in *mediation, family group conferencing, multidisciplinary team meetings* and any other formal or informal "out-of-court" opportunities to shape and achieve the father's goals. Encourage the father to participate as these approaches lead to higher reunification rates and greater satisfaction and sense of empowerment for families.

Absent Client

If the client cannot be found after the lawyer/client relationship is established, can you continue to represent the client? MR 1.2 lays out your obligation to pursue the goals of the client. The client sets the objectives of the litigation; you the lawyer determine the means.

How much can you assume to know about the intent of the client when your client cannot be reached? The analysis relates back to the section on appointment of counsel. It is a judgment call on your part. If you have had enough meaningful interaction before the client's disappearance, you may have enough information to continue to represent. If significant time has passed, or if little information was exchanged early on, the fact that the father once said "I don't want my parental rights terminated, and if they are, I'd like you to appeal" does not bind you to blindly pursue that goal. In fact, MR 1.2 and MR 3.1 suggest that without active, ongoing participation of the client, you may not be able to continue to represent him and/or file an appeal to a TPR judgment.[17]

If you have been in contact with your client, but he does not wish his whereabouts to be revealed, M.R. 1.6 requires you to keep that information confidential. If the court *orders* you to reveal your client's whereabouts, whether or not you do so requires a close look at MR 1.6. Under MR 1.6(b)(6), you *may* reveal otherwise confidential, protected information to "comply with a court order." However, under the Model Rules, this is a *permissive* circumstance under which confidential information can be revealed, so the choice is yours.[18]

Conflict of Interest

Can you represent the mother and nonresident father? What about representing different fathers when the case involves a sibling group? Prohibiting lawyers from representing clients when there is a conflict of interest is grounded in the notion that lawyers owe clients duties of loyalty, independent judgment, zealous pursuit of client objectives, and client confidentiality. When representing Client A compromises the duties the lawyer owes to Client B, there is a conflict. The key question is *whether zealously pursuing one client's objectives will prevent the lawyer from zealously pursuing another client's objectives, and whether confidentiality may be compromised.*

MR 1.7 strongly discourages dual representation. MR 1.7(a)(1) prohibits representing a client if that client's interests are *directly adverse* to another client, even if the matters are unrelated. This is because clients feel betrayed, and may fear the lawyer will pursue their case less effectively.[19] Even when there is no direct adverseness, representation is also prohibited under MR 1.7(a)(2) if there is a significant risk that the representation of one or more clients will be *materially limited* by the lawyer's responsibilities to another client, a former client, a third person, or by a personal interest of the lawyer. *The conflict forecloses alternatives that would otherwise be available to the client.*[20]

In most cases involving multiple children and multiple parents, the conflict is foreseeable and you should not accept appointment for two fathers.[21] For example, Father A may want custody of his child and Father B may want the mother to keep custody. Advocating on behalf of Father A may involve presenting evidence against the mother and arguing why she is inappropriate, and that may undermine the position of Father B. Further, confidential information about the mother, each father, or the children may be compromised when negotiating and advocating for the respective fathers.

Resources

➤ **Local Bar Association Ethics Hotlines.** In addition to consulting the Model Rules, you can contact your local bar ethics hotline for guidance.

➤ **National Project to Improve Representation for Parents Involved in the Child Welfare System**, a project of the ABA Center on Children and the Law, provides networking opportunities, a listserv, special events, and training and technical assistance for parents' lawyers. Visit www.abanet.org/child/parentrepresentation/home.html.

Clients can waive the potential conflict, even if it is foreseeable. Often, access to affordable counsel is a big issue for nonresident fathers, and is frequently the reason when they decide to waive conflicts of interest. If you represent multiple fathers and a conflict arises, whether you will need to withdraw from the case depends on the circumstances. If you can continue to preserve confidential communications, and zealously pursue each client's objectives, you may remain in the case. You must explain the potential conflict to each client, and each client must consent in writing.[22] Consent can be revoked any time.[23]

Conclusion

When representing nonresident fathers, you have an ethical responsibility to zealously advocate for your clients. This advocacy includes guiding fathers through the decision-making process so they can make informed decisions. It also involves regularly communicating with and apprising fathers of their choices and the effects and obligations surrounding each choice. Ethical challenges are bound to arise, including potential conflicts of interest, actions to take upon appointment, and methods for maintaining regular communication with the father. You can overcome these challenges and ensure the best possible advocacy for your client by consulting the guidance in the Model Rules.

Endnotes

1. All states have slightly different ethics rules, and while no state follows the Model Rules verbatim, the majority of states base their rules on the ABA Model Rules or the ABA Model Code of Professional Responsibility.

2. Sankaran, Vivek. "Procedural Injustice: How the Practices and Procedures of the Child Welfare System Disempower Parents and Why It Matters." *Michigan Child Welfare Law Journal*, Fall 2007.

3. This may be the shelter care hearing, 72-hour removal hearing, or other terminology to describe the initial hearing.

4. Cooper v. Salomon Bros., Inc., 1 F.3d 82 (2d Cir. 1993); Lynch v. Deaconess Medical Center, 776 P.2d 681 (Wash. 1989).

5. United States v. Weinstein, 511 F.2d 622 (2d Cir.1975).

6. In re Lieber, 442 A.2d 152 (D.C. 1982).

7. MR 1.3.

8. MR 1.4.

9. MR 1.2.

10. Ferri v. Ackerman, 444 U.S. 193 (1979); In re Lieber, 442 A.2d 152 (D.C. 1982).

11. MR 2.1.

12. MR 1.2.

13. MR 1.1, Comment 1.

14. ABA Standards of Practice for Attorneys Representing Parents in Abuse and Neglect Cases, available at: www.abanet.org/child/clp/ParentStds.pdf.

15. *See* Chapter 2, Kiselica, Mark S. "Understanding Male Help-Seeking Behaviors."

16. This advice needs to be balanced with advice that protects any competing client interests. For example, if the father is not seeking custody, or if there is a valid concern about potential criminal charges, it may be best to advise against cooperation with the agency. This is a difficult situation for any parent attorney as full cooperation with the agency can lead to a speedier reunification, but can also have potential harmful consequences that must be communicated and fully considered by the client.

17. MR 3.1 provides, in part, "A lawyer shall not bring or defend a proceeding, or assert ... an issue ..., unless there is a basis in law and fact for doing so that is not frivolous."

18. MR 1.6(b)(6). "A lawyer may reveal information relating to the representation of a client to the extent the lawyer reasonably believes necessary ... to comply with other law or court order."

19. MR 1.7, Comment 6.

20. MR 1.7, Comment 8.

21. MR 1.7, Comment 3.

22. MR 1.7(b)(4).

23. MR 1.7, Comment 21.

Appendices

Appendix A
Sample Questions and Checklist

Ask the following questions to assess whether your nonresident father client has established a constitutionally protected relationship with his child and what relationship he wants going forward.

Sample Questions to Ask the Father:

1. Is your name on the child's birth certificate?

2. Have you registered or filed your name in the paternity registry? (if applicable under state law)

3. Have you taken a paternity test?

4. (a) Have you ever lived with the mother? (b) For how long? (c) Before or after the child was born?

5. (a) Do you pay child support? (b) Have you ever?

6. Have you ever bought food, clothes, diapers, or other supplies for the child? When?

7. Do you send gifts or cards to your child(ren) on birthdays and holidays?

8. Do you visit with your child(ren) regularly?

9. Would you like to request that the court offer you (increased) visitation rights? (If yes, explain the possibilities of visitation that is unsupervised or only monitored.)

10. Do you or any of your family members ever take care of your child(ren) for any period(s) of time?

11. Are any of your relatives involved in your child(ren)'s life?

12. Do you speak to your child(ren) on the phone? How often?

13. Do you ever call or write to your child(ren)'s caregiver to ask about him/her (them)?

14. Do you attend doctor appointments, school conferences, or other activities for your child?

15. (a) Do you want custody of your child(ren) (b) What do you think you might need if (or before) you get custody (i.e., housing, job, parenting class, substance abuse treatment)?

16. What other steps would you like to take to establish a relationship with your child?

If the father has not been consistently involved…

17. Are there any reasons why you have not been more involved? Any circumstances or individuals that have made it difficult for you to establish a relationship with your child?

Use the following checklists to guide your advocacy for your nonresident father client.

Lawyer Checklist:

☐ Ask the father questions to determine his relationship/history with his children (see *Sample Questions* above).

☐ Know state process (e.g., registry, birth certificate) for protecting nonresident fathers' constitutionally protected interests.

☐ Understand the definition of a 'father' under state law and how to ensure your client meets that definition.

☐ Instruct and help your client file his name in the paternity registry (if applicable under state law).

☐ Request paternity testing early in the case and ensure the agency pays for it.

☐ If possible under state law, encourage him to have his name placed on the birth certificate retroactively.

☐ With client permission and if appropriate, request that the court offer him increased visitation rights and/or visitation that is unsupervised or only monitored (e.g., someone is not in the room with the father and child for the entire visit, but just checks in periodically).

Ongoing Tasks for Lawyers:

☐ Assess other steps your client may take to establish a relationship with the child.

☐ Ensure your client is aware of all important court dates at which he must appear.

☐ Be sure to work with the child welfare agency to involve your client and his family in case planning.

☐ Protect your client's constitutional rights during court proceedings.

Appendix B
Tips for the First Meeting with your Nonresident Father Client

1. Explain your role as the father's attorney for this case only—you represent no one else and are here specifically for his child welfare case.

2. Give a basic overview of how child welfare proceedings work in your jurisdiction and any acronyms or terminology he might hear and be unfamiliar with.

3. Explain how and when attorney-client privilege applies.

4. Exchange contact information. Explain the importance of staying in contact and how you will not be sharing his information with anyone unless he requests you do so. Ask him to give you several ways to reach him (e.g., home, work, and cell phone numbers; parents' or significant other's phone number).

5. Discuss any barriers that may prevent him from participating in the case:
    *   scheduling conflicts with work
    *   problems maintaining contact with counsel (e.g., he lacks a phone or stable housing)
    *   language barriers or literacy issues
    *   tension with the mother or maternal relatives
    *   transportation issues
    *   other ongoing legal proceedings or problems

6. Get his perspective on his child(ren), those involved in the case and allegations brought against him (if any).

7. Determine the client's legal status with respect to the child based on his account of the facts and relationship to his child(ren).

8. Ask if he has a job or other income, what his housing situation is, and if he's ever taken a parenting class and/or parented other children.

9. Obtain signed releases for medical and mental health records, school records, employment records, etc. Explain the potential use of this information by counsel.

10. Discuss his desires regarding the child's placement, visitation, and services for himself and the child.

11. Be straightforward about what he can realistically expect (e.g., If he's serving a lengthy jail sentence, will the court wait if he wants custody?).

12. Stress the father's responsibilities and his rights (e.g., paying child support, participating in services, visiting his child).

Appendix C
The Interstate Compact on the Placement of Children and Representing Nonresident Fathers

In many jurisdictions, the Interstate Compact on the Placement of Children ("ICPC") has been interpreted by child welfare agencies and courts to apply to out-of-state parents; this often includes nonresident fathers. If the ICPC is deemed to apply to nonresident parents, it requires the state where the nonresident parent lives to conduct a home study of the out-of-state placement and approve the placement before the state hearing the dependency case can place the child across state lines. Home studies can take months to complete, even if the child is only a few miles away from his nonresident parent seeking custody. If your nonresident father client is faced with this delay, consider the following to speed the process:

- Review the ICPC language and regulations to see whether any exceptions apply and whether any arguments can be made that applying the ICPC violates your client's constitutional rights.
- Determine whether the child may stay with the father on an extended visit pending completing the ICPC process.
- Determine whether you can request an expedited ICPC process from the agency or through the court.
- Assess whether you can arrange a home study through a private entity to accelerate the process.
- Coordinate with your client to ensure he timely completes his background paperwork.
- Review the sending agency's checklist of tasks to complete before forwarding information to the receiving state to track progress and ensure basic ICPC procedures are followed.
- Go over the home study criteria with your client in advance to see if he will run into any problems.
- Identify the ICPC administrators in the 'sending' and 'receiving' states to establish communication, track progress, and raise concerns when necessary.

Resources:

Sankaran, Vivek S. "Navigating the Interstate Compact on the Placement of Children: Advocacy Tips for Child Welfare Attorneys." *ABA Child Law Practice* 27(3), May 2008, 33.

Sankaran, Vivek S. "Out of State and Out of Luck: The Treatment of Non-Custodial Parents under the Interstate Compact on the Placement of Children." *Yale Law & Policy Review* 25, Fall 2006, 63.

Fiermonte, Cecilia. "Interstate Placements: Applying the ICPC." *ABA Child Law Practice* 21(5), July 2002, 65.

Appendix D

Your father clients need guidance to navigate the child welfare system. Use this handout to help each father understand his role in the process and how to help you advocate effectively for him. Take time to guide your father client through these tips, especially during your first meeting. Referring back to them throughout the case can reinforce them and help the father continue to use and follow them.

Ten Tips on How to Work With Your Lawyer

1. Be Honest

Your lawyer cannot tell anyone what you share with him unless you say it's OK. So, you should not be afraid to be open and honest with your lawyer about the facts of your case and be sure to share with him any information that may be brought up against you in court. Telling your lawyer everything that happened and relevant information about you, good and bad, will help him give you the right advice and make the best case for you in court. This may include information you have about how or whether your child was abused or neglected, whether you have a criminal history, or if you live with someone who the agency may not think should be around kids if you are asking for custody of your child.

2. Be Prepared

Ask your lawyer if you should take notes on the events that brought your child into the system and what happens during your case. Providing this information to your lawyer will allow her to be a better advocate for you. Each time before you meet with your lawyer, write down questions or issues you want to discuss with her. This will help your lawyer understand what is going on and what you want. Your lawyer is probably very busy with a lot of cases, so writing things down before you meet will give you a chance to discuss everything you want to cover. While it is important to be prepared and keep your lawyer informed about your case, you need to make sure you are also protecting the confidential relationship you have with your lawyer. Before you write down any notes or questions you have, make sure your lawyer knows you are recording this information. Also, do not share these written notes with anyone other than your lawyer.

3. Tell Your Lawyer What You Want to Happen

It is your lawyer's job to help you get what you want from the court and agency. This can include who you want your child to live with, how often you want to visit your child while she's in foster care, and what help or services you or your child need (e.g., transportation, job training, health care, etc.). Take your time and think about what you want for you and your child and share these goals with your lawyer. When you first meet with your lawyer, tell him your expectations and ask him what he will be able to do for you. He will ask you questions about your goals and give you advice on how best to achieve them. He will also give you feedback on whether your goals can be met and, if not, what else you should try.

4. Ask Questions

Ask your lawyer questions if you don't understand something. The court and child welfare systems can be confusing. It is important to understand these systems to achieve the result you want for you and your child.

5. Listen

Your lawyer will analyze the law and the information you gave her to give you legal advice on what she believes you should do. Listen carefully to this advice and decide if you want to follow it. Your lawyer has your best interests in mind. If you don't agree, tell your lawyer why, so the two of you can talk about your options.

6. Attend Out-of-Court Meetings

Ask your lawyer to go with you to important case planning and other meetings with the child welfare agency and other service providers. Your lawyer can advocate for you in these meetings and help make sure the agency provides you services to complete in a reasonable time. Try to get your lawyer's advice before you agree to participate in and complete services.

7. Keep in Touch

Make sure you have your lawyer's name, phone number, and address so you can contact him when there are new developments in your case or when you have questions or concerns. Try to meet with your lawyer before each court hearing to share what is happening in your case, the progress you have made with your case plan, and what you want to happen during the court hearing. Provide any important documents you have received from other parties since your last meeting. Make sure your lawyer has all of your contact information (address, cell phone, etc.), and let him know if you move or get a new phone number.

8. Keep Your Own File and Share Important Documents with Your Lawyer

Keep copies of all papers you get from anyone involved in your case. This includes orders from the court, any papers you get from your lawyer, and any documents you get from the agency or other service providers like a substance abuse program, parenting class, or job training program. When you start, make progress in, or complete a class or program, get a written record of this progress and share it with your lawyer.

9. Follow Up

If you have called your lawyer, but receive no response after a few days, don't be afraid to follow up. Leave another message with your phone number asking for a call back by a set time or write a letter. If you are not happy with how your lawyer is representing you, ask to meet to discuss your concerns. If you are still not happy with your lawyer's representation, ask your lawyer to withdraw as your counsel and ask the court to appoint a new lawyer. Child welfare cases move quickly and you may be required to do a lot in a short time. If you are not happy with the representation you are getting in court, express your concerns and resolve them quickly.

10. Speak the Same Language

If you are assigned a lawyer who speaks a different language than you, ask for an interpreter to attend all meetings between you and your lawyer so you can communicate and your lawyer can properly advise you.

Things to Bring When You Meet with Your Lawyer

- List of questions to ask or issues you want to discuss with your lawyer.
- Your notes of what has happened in your case since you last spoke with your lawyer. Your notes may cover things like your progress in finding housing, your contact with your children, and your attendance at agency meetings.
- Documents you have received since you last met with your lawyer (e.g., certificate from a parenting class, a letter from a caseworker, etc.)
- Your calendar, to schedule future meetings and confirm upcoming court dates.

Questions to Discuss with Your Lawyer

- What rights and responsibilities do I have as the child's father? What are my rights to see my child? What are my rights to know about and participate in court hearings for the abuse/neglect case?
- How long does my child have to stay in foster care? Can my child stay with me or one of my relatives?
- Is what I tell you kept secret? What information should I give you?
- What will you be able to help me with in the abuse/neglect case (placement, visitation, services, etc.)? Will you help me with other legal matters as well, like child support or a criminal case?
- How much can (or should) I talk to other people involved in the case (caseworker, mom's lawyer) when you aren't with me?
- How will becoming involved in the abuse/neglect case affect my child support obligations? How will getting partial custody or increased visitation affect them?

About the Authors

Andrew L. Cohen has represented parents and children for the Massachusetts Committee for Public Counsel Services Children and Family Law (CAFL) Division since 1995. As director of appeals at CAFL, he oversees the appellate panel, conducts trial and appellate trainings, and maintains a small trial and appellate caseload. He has argued many appeals before the Massachusetts Supreme Judicial Court and Appeals Court, and regularly files *amicus curiae* briefs in child welfare matters on behalf of his agency. He has authored articles and book chapters on evidence, parent representation, and child welfare trial and appellate practice. He currently serves on the steering committee for the ABA National Project to Improve Representation for Parents Involved in the Child Welfare System and on the Boston Bar Association ethics committee. He graduated from Harvard College and the University of Pennsylvania Law School.

Richard Cozzola is the supervising attorney of the Children's Law Project of the Legal Assistance Foundation of Chicago, which represents children, adolescents, and caregivers in juvenile court and child welfare matters and in special education and school discipline cases. Formerly, Mr. Cozzola was the program director of the Civitas ChildLaw Center at Loyola University Chicago; the deputy public guardian in charge and training director for the Cook County Public Guardian, Juvenile Division; and the supervising attorney of the Cabrini Green Legal Aid Clinic, where he represented adolescents involved in the juvenile and criminal court systems. He has extensive trial and appellate litigation experience in child welfare, adoption, and custody issues. Mr. Cozzola has been a faculty member and lecturer at state, national, and international child welfare legal training programs and conferences and has published on legal issues in child abuse and neglect and training child welfare professionals for court.

Kathleen Creamer is a staff attorney in the Family Advocacy Unit at Community Legal Services, Inc. (CLS) in Philadelphia, PA. Before joining CLS, Ms. Creamer was the director of legal services for Our Place in Washington, D.C. Our Place provides legal services in matters affecting women during and after incarceration, primarily in the areas of child custody, parole, medical treatment, and consequences of criminal conviction. Ms. Creamer clerked for Judge J. Michael Ryan of the District of Columbia Superior Court, Family Court. She received her B.A. from St. Mary's College of Maryland, and her J.D. from the University of North Carolina at Chapel Hill School of Law.

Judge Leonard P. Edwards (ret.) is a judge-in-residence with the California Administrative Office of the Courts, where he provides technical assistance to courts, particularly in areas involving children and families. Judge Edwards served for 26 years as a superior court judge in Santa Clara County, CA. He sat as a domestic relations judge and as a juvenile court judge. During his judicial career, he founded and was the first president of the Juvenile Court Judges of California. He also co-founded the Santa Clara County Domestic Violence Council, co-founded Kids In Common, and founded the Child Advocates of Santa Clara County. He was the President of the National Council of Juvenile and Family Court Judges in 2002-2003. He has taught at the University of Santa Clara Law School, Stanford Law School, and the California Judicial College and has provided judicial trainings in over 45 states and 8 countries. He has written widely, including the book, *Child Abuse and the Legal System*. Among his many awards, he received the 2004 William H. Rehnquist Award for Judicial Excellence.

Daniel L. Hatcher is an assistant professor of law at the University of Baltimore (UB) where he teaches the civil advocacy clinic, health care law, and a law and poverty seminar. His recent scholarship addresses conflicts between state agencies' revenue maximization strategies and the agencies' core missions to serve low-income children and families—including the practice of state foster care agencies converting foster children's social security benefits into state revenue, welfare cost-recovery policies in the TANF program, and foster care cost recovery through child support enforcement. Before joining the faculty at UB in 2004, Professor Hatcher was in a statewide position with the Maryland Legal Aid Bureau, serving as the assistant director of advocacy for public benefits and economic stability. He previously worked as a staff attorney for Legal Aid, representing abused and neglected children and representing adults in all areas of civil poverty law. He was also a senior staff attorney with the Children's Defense Fund's Family Income Division.

Dr. Mark S. Kiselica is a psychologist and professor of counselor education at The College of New Jersey. He is the author of over 120 publications, including five books, *Multicultural Counseling with Teenage Fathers* (Sage, 1995), *Handbook of Counseling Boys and Adolescent Males* (Sage, 1999), *Confronting Prejudice and Racism during Multicultural Training* (American Counseling Association, 1999), *Counseling Troubled Boys* (Routledge, 2008), and *When Boys Become Parents: Adolescent Fatherhood in America* (Rutgers University Press, 2008). He also is featured in the video, *Positive Psychology with Male Clients* (American Psychological Association, 2008). Dr. Kiselica is a fellow and former president of the Society for the Psychological Study of Men and Masculinity, a former consulting scholar for the Country Boys Community Engagement Outreach Campaign, and a member of the American Psychological Association Working Group to Develop Guidelines for Psychological Practice with Boys and Men. Currently, Dr. Kiselica is a member of the National Advisory Board for the National Quality Improvement Center on Non-Resident Fathers and the Child Welfare System, and he is the editor of the *Routledge Book Series on Counseling and Psychotherapy with Boys and Men*.

Jennifer L. Renne is assistant director of the National Child Welfare Resource Center for Legal and Judicial Issues at the ABA Center on Children and the Law. She conducts trainings for state court systems on child abuse and neglect, and researches and writes on child welfare issues. Jennifer co-authored *Making it Permanent: Efforts to Finalize Permanency Plans for Foster Children*, and authored *Legal Ethics in Child Welfare Cases* and *Child Safety: A Guide for Judges and Lawyers*. Jennifer represented children in child abuse and neglect cases for eight years at Maryland's Legal Aid Bureau, where she was supervising attorney of the child advocacy unit. She received her J.D. from Georgetown University Law Center and her B.A. from the University of Pennsylvania. She is an adjunct professor at Georgetown University Law Center, teaching professional responsibility to public interest law students.

Vivek S. Sankaran is a clinical assistant professor of law in the Child Advocacy Law Clinic at the University of Michigan Law School. He previously represented children, parents, and caregivers in child abuse and neglect matters for The Children's Law Center in Washington, D.C. His research and policy interests center on improving outcomes for children in child abuse and neglect cases by empowering parents and strengthening due process protections in the child welfare system. Professor Sankaran sits on the Steering Committee of the ABA National Project to Improve Representation for Parents Involved in the Child Welfare System and chairs the Michigan Court Improvement Project subcommittee on parent representation. He has also authored scholarly pieces and practical resource guides to assist professionals working with parents in the system and regularly conducts national and statewide trainings on these issues. He received his J.D. from the University of Michigan Law School, and his B.A. from the College of William and Mary.

Andrya L. Soprych is a social worker at the Legal Assistance Foundation of Metropolitan Chicago (LAF). She began working there in February of 2007. Ms. Soprych is a Licensed Social Worker and received her MSW from the Jane Addams College of Social Work at University of Illinois at Chicago (UIC) with a concentration in Children and Families. She is a field instructor for the University of Chicago's, Loyola's, and UIC's graduate schools of social work.

NATIONAL QUALITY IMPROVEMENT CENTER
ON NON-RESIDENT FATHERS AND THE CHILD WELFARE SYSTEM

Visit our Web site for More Resources!
www.fatherhoodqic.org

Visit the National Quality Improvement Center on Non-Resident
Fathers and the Child Welfare System (QIC-NRF) Web site
for additional resources to help legal professionals better
engage fathers in child welfare case plans and hearings.

Resources include:

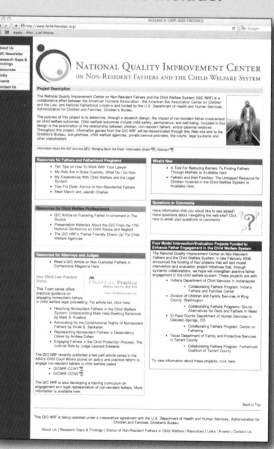

➤ Resources aimed at fathers to **share with your clients**

➤ The latest research and findings related to nonresident fathers involved in the child welfare system, including a comprehensive **literature review**

➤ The latest QIC NRF **products and publications**

➤ A **training curriculum** for attorneys representing nonresident fathers in child welfare matters

➤ Contact information for project staff who can provide **training** and other resources

➤ The project's quarterly **newsletter**, including a **special issue on fathers and the courts**

Visit us today at
www.fatherhoodqic.org